You're Going To Die... But Not Me!

A
Psychologist
Wrestles Death

Liz Scott, Ph.D.

"A deliciously pointed investigation of not-being from one of my favorite thinkers."

   —**Laura Stanfill**
      Author of *Imagine a Door*

"A perfectly balanced, harmonious, touching and uplifting book about our most haunting issue: death. Only Liz Scott could write a book about death that will leave you howling. I laughed to the point of tears at her wry observations, morbid humor—and touching humanity. You could die laughing, right? Well, this is the book that will get you there. Highly recommend it."

   —**Rene Denfeld**
      Bestselling author of *The Enchanted* and *The Child Finder*

"In this memoir/essay collection, Scott looks at death from every conceivable angle...slicing and dicing away in an attempt to alleviate her fear. With humor injected into every open crevice, this is a must-have book for anyone who might die. Highly recommended."

   —Jennifer Pastiloff
   Bestselling author of ***On Being Human***

"A Witty and Poignant Meditation on Mortality. Rarely does a book about death manage to be as life-affirming, insightful, and, dare I say, laugh-out-loud funny as You're Going to Die.. But I'm Not by Liz Scott, PhD. With a sharp wit and a keen eye for the absurdities of existence, Scott takes readers on a journey through the complexities of mortality, grief, and the various ways we attempt to make sense of and live with the inevitable.

Each essay is a gem, filled with sharp observations, personal anecdotes, and a voice that is as engaging as it is wise. She has a gift for finding light in the darkest corners and I recognized my own feelings and ponderings on every page.

Highly recommended for anyone who enjoys smart, darkly humorous writing with a big beating heart at its center."

   —Shavaun Scott
   Author of ***Nightbird***

"Liz Scott takes us on an unflinching, deeply personal, and unexpectedly witty journey into the heart of our greatest fear—death. With warmth, vulnerability, and a sharp eye for the absurd, she transforms existential dread into something intimate, meaningful, and even—dare I say—comforting. This book isn't just about dying; it's about how we live, what we leave behind, and the stories that tether us to one another. A must-read for anyone seeking a deeper understanding of mortality and the meaning we make along the way."

> —**Shoshana Ungerleider, MD,**
> Founder, **End Well**; Producer & Host, ***TED Health***

"In You're Going to Die..But I'm Not by Liz Scott, Ph.D. Scott turns death, her fear of death, over and around and up and down. In this smart, funny, personal collection, Scott invites us into her deep and wide inquiry. Sometimes the easiest way into the dark is with humor and a reliable lantern. Scott's exploration of death through history, philosophy, religion, fear and more, all with a sidecar of humor, leaves room for us to be curious about our own fears and beliefs around death. We're all going to die. Oh, except Scott. Highly recommend."

> —**Anne Gudger**
> Author of ***The Fifth Chamber***

"The world would be a better place if everyone used their fear of death as the springboard to create something as thoughtful, profound, and witty as Liz Scott has. You're Going to Die..But I'm Not is part research project, part intimate conversation, and part wise meditation on life's greatest mystery. It left me wanting to write more, read more, talk more about everything that matters."

  —**Michelle Wildgen**
    Author of ***Wine People***

"There is no end to books with prescriptive wisdom on how to live a better life. But what about the other side of the life-and-death binary? Liz Scott has written an unflinching treatise that explores the taboo subject of death. You're Going to Die..But I'm Not is an impeccably researched book acknowledging the fears, questions, and anxieties in the face of inevitable mortality. And like any worthwhile writing about death, it's sprinkled with gallows humor."

  —**Suzy Vitello**
    Author of ***Bitterroot*** and ***The Bequest***

"If you think you're the world champion of existential dread, I have bad news: Liz Scott has you beat. The good news is that she was kind enough to take us with her as she wrestled her demons, using tools from ancient wisdom to modern psychedelics and more. Her writing is smart, witty and always incisive. The best part, tho? This book legit made me feel less dread about someday being dead. That, my friend, is miraculous."

—**Courtenay Hameister**
　Author of ***Okay Fine Whatever***

Copyright © 2026 • All Rights Reserved
Liz Scott, Ph.D.
Pierian Springs Press

Other than review quotes or academic excerpts,
no part of this work may be reproduced
without explicit permission.

First printing, May 2026
Library of Congress Control Number: pending
ISBN 978-1-965784-36-5 Hardback
ISBN 978-1-965784-37-2 Paperback
Printed in the United States of America, Canada, Australia,
Saudi Arabia, Japan, India, Brazil, and the European Union

Book Design & Typography by **Kurt Lovelace**
Cover art *War or the Ride of Discord* by **Henri Rousseau**
Cover type *Bauhaus Dessau* **Alfarn** by Céline Hurka,
Elia Preuss, Flavia Zimbardi,
Hidetaka Yamasaki, and Luca Pellegrini.
Editor name in **Jenson** by Robert Slimbach.
Back Cover names in **Gill Sans Nova**.
Titles and body text set in **Baskerville**.
Flourishes set in Emigre Foundry **Dalliance** by Frank Heine.
Emigre Foundry **ZeitGuys** by Bob Aufuldish, Eric Donelan.
Typefaces licensed Adobe, Linotype, Emigre, & URW
GmbH.

PierianSpringsPress.Com
Pierian Springs Press, Inc
30 N Gould St, Ste 25398
Sheridan, Wyoming 82801-6317

For Robert and Bridget and Will
who live on

Contents

Prologue | v

1 | Memento–As if I Could Forget–Mori | 1
2 | Don't Be Like Susan | 7
3 | At the Bookstore | 11
4 | This is How I Will Die | 17
5 | Terror Management Theory | 23
6 | Stealing From Maggie Smith | 27
7 | Regrets, I've Had a Few | 29
8 | This Body of Mine | 35
9 | St. Joseph, My Man | 47
10 | Don't Forget Me | 49
11 | Death Attitude Profile, Revised | 51
12 | Reading Dylan Thomas | 57
13 | Living Like Emily | 61
14 | Maneki-neko | 67
15 | Mediums & Psychics & Channelers, OhMy! | 69
16 | What's the Alternative? | 79
17 | My Dog Billy | 81
18 | You Sure Look Like My Mother But... | 89
19 | Reading List | 95
20 | NDE. Yes, Please | 97

21 | Talking to Angels | 111
22 | Lesson Learned | 119
23 | Closest I've Come For Real | 125
24 | Just Say Yes! | 127
25 | Me in the Corner, Choosing My Religion | 141
26 | I, it Seems, am a Hungry Ghost | 159
27 | Famous, Albeit Ostensible, Last Words | 167
28 | Nothing New Under the Sun | 177
29 | Hello Darkness, My New Friend | 181
30 | Relationship Status | 189

AFTERWORD | 193

 ACKNOWLEDGEMENTS | 195

 ABOUT THE AUTHOR | 197

You're Going To Die... But Not Me!

PROLOGUE

"I had a stick of CareFree gum, but it didn't work. I felt pretty good while I was blowing that bubble, but as soon as the gum lost its flavor, I was back to pondering my mortality."
   –Mitch Hedberg

Scholars date the earliest recorded history as primarily from Mesopotamia and Egypt, sometime between 3400-3200 BCE. And from this history, there is evidence that the pursuit of eternal life might just be the ultimate and persistent, albeit quixotic, quest. The ankh ☥, a symbol of immortality, appeared in Egypt right around that point in human history. What followed were countless symbols of eternal life across all cultures of the known world. Among them are:

- 🔥 The phoenix
- 🔥 The eternal flame
- 🏵 The peacock
- 🪷 The lotus flower

vi • *Prologue*

- ☆ The north star
- 🌲 Evergreens
- ▲ The pyramids
- 🪲 The scarab
- 🍑 The peach
- ∞ The infinity sign
- ⭕ The circle
- 🍄 The reishi mushroom
- 🕊 The dove
- ꩜ The knot of eternity

And, among all the many more too numerous to name, the list also includes the laurel, Tithonus, Ouroboros, Shouxing, mistletoe, amaranth, Kalasha, corals, the heart-leaved moonseed, wisteria, Kanatitsa, Idun, and the crane.

The search for immortality, it seems, is as old as time and as new as five minutes ago. The *Epic of Gilgamesh* is a Mesopotamian epic poem, originating from around 2100 BCE—which is widely recognized as the oldest surviving literary work. The main theme of this ancient text is the hero's quest for immortality. "Must I die too?" Gilgamesh cries to the heavens.

Qin Shi Huang, the first emperor of China, ruled in the 3rd century B.C. Along with creating the famous Terracotta Army which you may have seen when it toured many museum in the U.S., he was the first man to conquer the seven kingdoms of ancient China and proceed to rule them all. There was only one threat left for him to overcome: death itself. To this formidable and mighty emperor, death was unthinkable, and he was hell-bent on living forever. He outlawed the discussion of death at court under penalty of—blind to the irony, I guess—death. The story goes that he was so obsessed with this irrational quest that, when he heard of graffiti prophesying that he too would eventually die, he demanded to know who had written it; and when no one came forward, he had every single person in the area executed.

The *Rigveda*, the ancient Indian collection of Vedic Sanskrit hymns, describes Soma as the elixir of immortality. Considered the most precious liquid in the universe, the belief was that the gods consumed massive quantities of Soma to ensure their immortality: "We have drunk Soma and become immortal. We have attained the light the gods discovered. Now what may foeman's malice do to harm us? What, O Immortal, can mortal man's deception do?"

In Greek mythology, Prometheus defies the gods by stealing fire for humanity, which symbolizes a challenge to the divine order and represents an attempt to transcend human limitations—primarily the ultimate limitation: death.

And then there is Medea. Her story is complex and, in some accounts, contradictory. In one version of the myth, in an attempt to make her children immortal, she buries them in the sanctuary of Hera, only to have them die from, well, being buried. In some texts, Medea is said to have eventually achieved immortality herself, going on to reside perpetually in the Elysian Fields, which, in Greek mythology, is the afterlife paradise.

In Goethe's *Faust*, the protagonist makes a pact with the devil to gain knowledge and experience, all in an effort to escape the limitations of human existence. And what, you might ask, is the ultimate limitation? Death, of course.

In Oscar Wilde's *The Picture of Dorian Gray*, the

protagonist remains forever youthful while his portrait—which he stashes away in an attic so it will never be seen—reveals all the marks of aging and sin. This, of course, is a deluded example of the denial of the natural aging process, which implies the even more deluded notion that one might be able to attain everlasting life.

In Bram Stoker's *Dracula*, Count Dracula in the embodiment of an undead being, and, of course, being undead means living forever.

Damien Hirst often uses themes of death and immortality in his art. His 1991 *The Physical Impossibility of Death in the Mind of Someone Living* is an installation which features a preserved shark in formaldehyde. In this controversial piece, Hirst implies that the shark is simultaneously life and death incarnate, a nod to everlasting life...and perhaps also to Erwin Schrödinger.

Darren Aronofsky's 2006 film *The Fountain* intertwines three narratives across time, focusing on the quest for eternal life and the challenge of accepting mortality.

And then there is this from Woody Allen: "I don't want to achieve immortality through my work; I want to achieve immortality through not dying..."

Of course, these are but a tiny few. I could get forever lost in the superfluity of examples from the beginning of recorded history up until the day you are reading this.

What is undeniably true is that at every point in history, the quest for immortality has been an obsession for us humans. And furthermore, in pursuit of this quest, it seems there is no end to how we will try *not* to die. We've used elixirs, hormones, prayers, pills, spells, and stem cells. We've resorted to eating mummies, buzzard stones, jade, and pulverized boar penises. We've injected ourselves with extracts from the testicles of guinea pigs and dogs. We've ingested liquid mercury and gold.

Check this out. This was the *Time Magazine* cover of September 30, 2013, about a Google-invested biotech company Calico. According to the article, Calico "...is spending untold amounts on a project that flies in the face of the human condition, the existential certainty of aging and death."

Finally, as I was finishing this chapter, I came across an article that was just published in *The New Yorker*. In *How to Live Forever and Get Rich Doing It,* Tad Friend explores a movement—especially among the uber-wealthy—to engage in some pretty wacky-sounding efforts to crack the mortality code, including harnessing the power of A.I. to find a fix for debility and death. Or, instead of waiting for that, you might decide, as some of these folks do, to take rapamycin, a drug derived from bacterium discovered on Easter Island. Many of the efforts among this cohort fall under the rubric of *longevity escape velocity* which posits that medical and scientific advances in the area of life-extension will progress so rapidly that our lifespan will just continue to expand and expand and.........

1

MEMENTO–AS IF I COULD FORGET–MORI

This might be an apocryphal story. I hope not, especially since it gives me a hit of schadenfreude. In ancient Rome, generals victorious in battle would parade through the streets while slaves walked closely behind them, their sole responsibility throughout the entire procession being to continuously whisper in the general's ear, "*Respice post te. Hominem te esse memento. Memento mori!*," which roughly translates to, "Look behind. Remember thou art mortal. Remember you must die!"

Talk about a buzzkill! Just at the point when you feel all puffed up by success, flaunting yourself among the adoring hoi polloi, a slave—of *all* people—brings you back down to earth. Gotta say, if I were one of those slaves, that would be a bright spot in what I'm betting is my miserable existence.

So mine is a kind of schadenfreude by proxy, I guess.

The phrase *memento mori* probably has its origins in ancient Rome and Greece, where it was common for people to carry small tokens or talismans—often in the form of a skull or skeleton—that served as reminders of death. These were worn as symbols of the fragility of life, especially during times of war, when death could come at any moment. Or, indeed, at any other time, when death could also come at any moment.

The Stoics were big proponents of this admonition. For example:

Seneca: *"Let us prepare our minds as if we'd come to the very end of life. Let us postpone nothing. Let us balance life's books each day..."*

Marcus Aurelius: *"You could leave life right now. Let that determine what you do and say and think."*

Epictetus: *"Keep death and exile before your eyes each day, along with everything that seems terrible—by doing so, you'll never have a base thought nor will you have excessive desire."*

Socrates: *"The one aim of those who practice philosophy in the proper manner is to practice for dying and death."*

And perhaps my most favorite quote, attributed to Epicurus: *"Non Fui, Fui, Non-sum, Non-curo,"* which roughly translates to, "I was not, I was, I am not, I do not care."

And, of course, I'm not stopping with the Stoics.

In ancient Egypt, feasts were often concluded by raising a toast to a skeleton: "Drink and be merry, for such shalt thou be when thou are dead."

During the late-middle ages in Europe, the artistic genre of *danse macabre* depicts people from all social classes being carried off by the grim reaper.

In Japanese culture, cherry blossoms and their short bloom represent the fleeting nature of life.

The Mexican festival *Day of the Dead* often includes skull-shaped candies and loaves of bread decorated with bread "bones."

In Tibetan Buddhism, *lojong* is a contemplative practice that includes a nine-point meditation on death, encompassing concepts such as the inevitability of death and the uncertainty of how and when one will die.

Sufis are sometimes called *ahl al-qubur* or "people of the graves" based on their practice of visiting graveyards as a reminder of mortality.

In Iceland, there is a gnomic poem attributed to the god Odin which says, in part: "Animals die, friends die, and thyself, too, shall die."

The Capela dos Ossos in Évora, Portugal, is a chapel whose walls are covered with human bones and skulls.

Then there is this from the Book of Ecclesiastes in the Bible: "This is the evil in everything that happens under the sun: The same destiny overtakes all. The hearts of people, moreover, are full of evil and there is madness in their hearts while they live, and afterward they join the dead."

Mindfulness of death is a central teaching in Buddhism. The meditative practice *maranasati*, meaning "death awareness," is considered essential to better living. It brings recognition to the transitory nature of our physical lives and asks us to consider whether we are making the right use of what Mary Oliver calls our "... one wild and precious life." As the Buddha put it: "Of all the footprints, that of the elephant is supreme. Similarly, of all mindfulness meditation, that on death is supreme."

Back when I practiced yoga for two seconds, we ended each class in *savasana*, or corpse pose. This, we were told, was a time to unwind our body and mind and to integrate what we got (or, in my case, didn't get) from the previous poses we did (or, in my case, attempted to do and failed at). It turns out, though, that the ancient yogis were not that concerned with relaxation.

Savasana—also known as *mrtasana*—was seen as a way to practice death, especially through the death of desire and grasping, and then ultimately of your life on this planet. The idea is that if we experience how peaceful non-existence is, we will no longer fear the real thing; that in corpse pose we can feel the separation of our body from our spirit (if you say so); and that knowing we will someday leave our bodies permanently, our spirit—which is our true self and isn't attached to our body—will endure (o-kay). I guess this is what helps us accept our mortality.

Oh, Buddha, you make it sound so easy!

I can't say I derived much of that particular benefit while lying in corpse pose, but it sure was my favorite part of class!

The *memento mori* admonition—advice, counsel, suggestion—can be found all over the place: in The Bible, in Shakespeare, in *Fahrenheit 451*, on YouTube, and in the paintings and sculptures at the Louvre and every other museum in the world, to mention just a few among more than I could ever name. Once you start looking for them, you will see countless images of skulls, hourglasses, skeletons, and pieces of mourning jewelry. Death is in our faces everywhere, *ad*—practically—*infinitum*. Antiquity and modernity are riddled with philosophers wagging their fingers at us to remember that we are mortal, that time's a-tickin' and that we'd better *carpe* the hell out of the *diem*.

Bottom line is this: No one has to tell me to *memento mori*. I'd actually like five minutes or so when I didn't have to *memento* it. That said, as much as this project has me swimming in all things death, it is also comforting to see that I am far from alone in this obsession of mine. In fact, from what read, it was way back in the Paleolithic era—2.5 to 3 million years ago—that early humans began to understand the concept of death and developed beliefs about an afterlife. And with the development of language and then the written word, our species has been—to cop to my own state of mind—obsessed.

Not that any of this is a surprise to me. I'm a person who thinks about death approximately 20 to 30 times a day. And it is simply not possible to believe that I am alone in the way I relate to my mortality. What is hard to believe is that some people don't even give it a second thought. Or, if they do, they only think about it every now and then. And even at those occasional times when they do, they just shrug their shoulders about it all.

If that's you, please tell me how. I'm here with an open mind, waiting for your wisdom.

2

DON'T BE LIKE SUSAN

Susan Sontag was terrified of dying. And I mean terri-fied. Don't take it from me.

This from Katie Roiphe's beautiful book, *The Violet Hour*: "If there is anyone on earth who could decide not to die, it would be Susan Sontag: her will is that ferocious, that unbending, that unwilling to accept the average fates or outcomes the rest of us are bound by."

Sontag's son, David Rieff, gives us even more insight into her feelings related to her mortality in his book *Swimming in a Sea of Death: A Son's Memoir*. In vivid detail, he recounts his mother's fierce battle with repeated bouts of cancer and her even fiercer attempts to deny her impending death. He writes, "So terrified of death that she could not bear to speak of it, my mother was also obsessed with it... She was an inveterate visitor of cemeteries. And she kept a human skull on the ledge behind her work table, nestled among the photographs of writers she admired (there were no family pictures)..."

Obsessed and terrified. ME TOO, SUSAN! (Except I don't have a skull, and I do have family pictures.)

I think I must have made this up because I've scanned the internet, googling *Susan Sontag death, Susan Sontag last days in hospital, Susan Sontag on hospital gurney, Susan Sontag freaking out*—and I keep coming up empty.

It seems I have an apparent fiction of my own mind that in her final days, in the throes of her panic about her death, as the orderly wheeled her down the hospital corridor, she stretched out her bone-thin arms, feebly trying to reach the walls, delusionally believing that if she could just keep the gurney from moving—keep it from getting her to that next place, a place where she would meet her demise—if she could stop the forward motion, then she would not die.

I must have made that up.

Or projected myself onto that scene—which now that I think about it, probably makes much more sense. I must have layered my own fear on top of hers and created this image of pathos—a dying woman so deluded that she believed if she could just keep herself from moving ten feet down the corridor, then she would not die.

After her last and final cancer diagnosis, Sontag turned her apartment into research central, and this is a gambit that I can totally relate to. When my young and healthy and strapping husband was diagnosed with stomach cancer—which, by the way, was in the days when it wasn't so blazingly easy to search every arcane corner of the internet—that's exactly what I did: I turned my home into research central.

Oh, the lengths I went to!

Even though the oncologist suggested that we might best spend our time "Going to Tahiti," I was beyond determined to scour every possible medical journal I could get my hands on, even managing to obtain access to the Oregon Health and Sciences University Medical School archives. A damn dog with a damn bone I was, bound and determined to uncover any new treatments, clinical trials, quack cures, and world experts whom I then went on to contact—which even required paying for a Japanese translator to sit by my side as I held telephone appointments with doctors in Tokyo.

Yes, in spite of the very thinly veiled and easily decoded prognosis that we "go to Tahiti," I spent that precious time—time which might have been better spent meditating on acceptance, backing away from the computer, or even fucking going to fucking Tahiti—instead, I spent that time in some frantic, futile, and deluded hunt.

So yes, Susan. I feel you. And yet, there's a strange way in which steeping myself in Sontag's story functions as a cautionary tale. What a horrifying and—sorry, Susan—pathetic picture the story of her relationship to her death paints for me.

No, I do not want to inflict the trauma I imagine befell her son onto my own children.

No, I do not want to end my life in a state of bizarre delusion.

No, I do not want to fritter away what might be my scant remaining time in anxiety and terror.

No, I do not want to be like Susan.

I'd rather go to Tahiti.

3

AT THE BOOKSTORE

Dear Mr. Ostaseski:
I was so excited to hear that you would be doing a reading at Powell's bookstore here in Portland. I just knew that your latest book, *The Five Invitations: Discovering What Death Can Teach Us About Living Fully*, would be exactly what I needed to help me with my anxiety about my ever-nearing demise. You must have sat with hundreds of people at the Zen Hospice Guest House, maybe thousands. I know you were the founder of that amazing project. And then there's your experience with the Metta Institute and its focus on end-of-life issues. I imagine you must know more about death that just about anyone.

I am sure you can understand why I was so hopeful.

Don't get me wrong. I have the very deepest respect and admiration for you and all the good work you have done in the world. Awed I am and humbled by my puny life in comparison.

But—

My fear wasn't quelled, not even a little. Truth is, my

anxiety might even have ticked up a notch after I left the reading.

The part I can get behind with no reservation is your subtitle: *Discovering What Death Can Teach Us About Living Fully.* This is what we've got, so let's make the most of it. And, of course, people like Viktor Frankl posited that it is death that gives our life meaning. Or Camus, who believed that facing up to the inevitability of our own death can help us appreciate the value of our lives.

Yes, yes, yes.

Keeping death on your shoulder has always been a concept that makes sense to me. But keeping death on my *alive* shoulder is one thing. You know, the shoulder that's on my alive, walking-around body. That I can do, no problem. It's what you went on to say at the reading.

Please forgive me if this is an overly simplified and, who knows, maybe not even accurate distillation of your message. Tell me if I'm wrong, but this is what I heard you say: The antidote to the fear of dying is to live a full life.

No, no, no, and HARD NO!

It's very difficult for me to believe that I'm the only one who feels this way, but living a full life makes me *more* afraid of dying. I do have a full life, and precisely because I do, I! Do! Not! Want! To! Leave! It!

You yourself certainly seem to have a rich and exceedingly rewarding life. All the people you help, all the fascinating colleagues you have. And such meaningful work. I can only imagine. I do wish I understood how equanimous you are—or appear to be anyway—at the notion of losing it all. Do you have a family? Friends?

When I think of leaving my daughters and my grandson—of never hearing Ashley laugh her winsome laugh or listen to Erica belt a song; never watch Milo do a Rubik's cube in 20 seconds or fling a frisbee at the coast. When I think of the birthday dinners, squeezing extra folding chairs around the table that I once thought was big enough but really is not; and our Thanksgiving alphabet tradition: I'm thankful for <u>A</u>musement Parks, I'm grateful for <u>B</u>acon, I'm thankful for <u>C</u>ats, thank God for <u>D</u>ecaf, and on and on until someone struggles to find something besides <u>Z</u>ebras to be thankful for. How in God's green earth do you leave all that?

Sometimes I hear people express a worry that they will never accomplish what they need to before their time on this earthly plane is over. This they connect with a fear of dying. It's almost the opposite of my fear of leaving a full life, don't you think? I cannot relate. It's true, I've never been a person of great ambition. There are precious few goals I've felt compelled to meet, no missions that have been driving forces, no Mt. Olympus to summit. Yes, I did get a Ph.D. and for sure that's a mountain to climb. But you might be shocked to know just how little thought went into embarking on that whole path. My life, it seems, has been a matter of simply taking the next logical step. The story of my life: put one foot down after the last.

So when my friend says, "I'm afraid I won't accomplish all I want to before I die," I say, "Hmmmm, that never even crossed my mind!" Although, now that I think about it, maybe not entirely opposite after all. I will, in fact, be disappointed if I never have the chance to see the animals in Africa. I've wanted to do that since forever. Or the dream of living for a year in Paris. Another lifelong obsession. The thing is, though, in no way do I attach these minor missed opportunities to the thought or fear of my mortality. If these opportunities never come to pass, I will have mild regrets. They would be disappointments that I can totally live with—emphasis on *live*.

Mr. Ostaseski, I am curious. Do you believe in life after death? My layperson's understanding of Buddhist philosophy is that life and death are a continuum, that we go through countless cycles of birth, death, and rebirth—the *samsara*. But I don't think that means Frank continues to be Frank; that whatever the next incarnation is, that it/he/she will be imbued with Frank's personality; that there is a "Frankness" that endures. Do you?

I know there are supposedly sane people who are actually excited about what they think of as the "next adventure." Some say those were Timothy Leary's last words before he died—but once a psychologist, always a psychologist. I just file that under a defense mechanism to contend with the terror, something we in the trade might call a counter-phobic response.

And then there's my late friend Bridget—a wiser, more grounded, and more intelligent person you'd never meet. She died convinced that she would be reuniting with her late husband, Chuck, in the afterlife. Not his spirit, not his essence, not his molecules—the actual 5'11", blue-eyed, blond him. She had no reason to fear death. Lucky her. How I wish I could get there. But you just can't make yourself buy that, can you? You can't jigsaw that piece in where it doesn't fit. Let me tell you, I've tried. The best I can do is say, okay, very true, I do believe that anything is possible. But I can barely hide my eyeroll, even to myself.

I am beginning to think that I have much more work to do on my spiritual, emotional, and psychological self than I have thought.

I've been a psychologist for over 45 years and have worked with hundreds upon hundreds of people, digging the depths. And when you dig the depths with a client, you're almost always digging your own depths as well. It's true for me, anyway. And especially in the last few decades, I have prided myself on my dedication to growth. I have intended to keep a keen eye on my moral inventory (if a non-addict may borrow this phraseology), and am committed to being open to explore all sorts of areas I may earlier have scoffed at. You'd think that would help. It seems, from where you stand—and I truly do bow down to your wisdom—I have a lot more work to do.

So, Mr. Ostaseski, can you help me?

Sincerely,
Still afraid in Portland

4

THIS IS HOW I WILL DIE

I'm thinking there might be something wrong with my throat.

Here's just one example out of so many I could list. Someone I know won an Oscar and every year after she was allowed to bring one guest to the Academy Awards. One happy and very lucky year I was that guest. Anyone who knows me would have no problem understanding. The fucking Academy Awards!

I shopped for the perfect dress. I reserved a room just across the street from the venue about a year ahead of time. I lost weight. I got my hair cut. I imagined I was a star and wrote an acceptance speech.

The day finally arrives and about two hours before the pre-show red carpet doings, I start to prep. A long, relaxing bath spiked with lavender oil. More time than I have ever taken on my hair and make-up, more than even on my wedding day(s). I slip into the long, fire engine red dress with the slit up the front of the right leg. Put on my strappy heels and crystal chandelier earrings. Ten minutes to relax and yes, I'm ready for my close-up, Mr. DeMille.

I have one foot right over the threshold and, damn, the phone rings. A nurse is calling me from a hospital in San Francisco. My mother is there, at the hospital. The nurse tells me that things don't look good. She says your mother is in severe pain, the worst of her life, that's what your mother is saying, and we're waiting for the test results but she doesn't look good. She is moaning and incoherent. She keeps saying she wants you to come. She says you should get here as soon as you can. She says she knows "this is the end."

And of course I will go because what if she dies and I don't see her and she knows I chose the Oscars over her and I can't hold her hand and she goes to her death ruined by her failures as a parent and I have to live with my failures as a daughter and we don't find any comfort with each other and neither one of us ever feels the solace of absolution.

In the space of ten minutes, I have taken off my dress–the fire engine red one with the slight up the front–thrown it into my suitcase with the rest of my crap, called the airline, checked out of the hotel, summoned a taxi, and *Driver, LAX, step on it*!

The television is on in my mother's room, loud enough that I can hear it before I get very close. I'm breathless from hustling through two airport terminals and down the long hospital corridor and before I even step inside her room I can hear Jon Stewart winding up his opening shtick.

My mother is sitting up in bed, sipping on the tiny straw of a cranberry cocktail juice box, wearing a T-shirt that says Gucci in gold letters, and she is very definitely alive. Her hair, ravaged by decades of perms and dye-jobs from platinum to raven black, now looking strangely like the color of circus peanuts.

She is tickled pink to see me. "Lizzie," she says, waving her hand wildly at the TV. "I saw you in the crowd, on the red carpet thing, I told the nurse, that's my daughter!"

Yeah, well, here's the thing. You did *not* just see me on the red carpet thing because it was happening exactly while I was harping at the cab driver to go faster, faster because I had to rush to make the god-damn flight so I could harp at another cab driver to go faster, faster so I could run practically out of breath down two airport terminals and the long hospital corridor and make it to the bedside of my dying mother.

You do not get to rip me away from the Oscars and get bragging rights about *look that's my daughter on the red carpet* too. You have to choose, woman! You don't get to pull one of your famous double binds on me, not today, not now, not again, no!

The flight home is a hot mess nightmare. I'm standby so what I get is just about the last row, middle seat. It's a pouring down monster storm. Thunder and lightning flashes cut the night sky. The plane is lurching so much that the man next to me–who might also have something wrong with his throat– clamps my arm, this close to drawing blood and proceeds to vomit. I'm scared too, of course, but my fear seems somehow blunted, probably pushed to the side by the sack of all the other feelings I'm hauling home. There just is not any room left for the panic I would normally be feeling. Mostly I'm numb.

When we finally land, the plane erupts in the applause of relief. Yeah, I'm relieved too. I guess. Hard to tell. Outside, I can barely muster the energy to lift my arm to hail a cab in what continues to be a deluge. On the way home the cab hydroplanes across the Fremont Bridge. At least that's what it feels like. Again, under usual circumstances this would be a fist-clenching, rapid-heart-beating, foot-jamming-into-pretend-brakes-in-the-backseat kind of experience that would send me almost over the edge to a full-blown panic attack but, instead, I'm kind of complacent, weirdly relaxed, or maybe just too empty to give a shit. Visibility is about zero and lightning flashes perilously close to the bridge, again that's what it looks like, and when the cabby finally pulls up in front of my building, I'm not even sure if I have what it takes to open the door.

Maybe I'll just live in the back seat of the cab. Lie down and call it a day. But I manage to make it out, lug my suitcase packed with that red hot slinky dress with the slit up the right leg into the building, and ride the elevator up to my floor.

I have not been to the Academy Awards, I have not worn my red dress and my mother is still alive. But right now, all that matters is finally making it to the quiet, uncomplicated, non-gaslight-y, simply-me-and-mine sanctuary that is my home. I have never been so happy to turn the key in my front door. Relieved? For sure. But my body is vibrating from exhaustion, anger and oh, yes—hunger. No food since, since? Since when? Since before the red dress with the slit up the leg. Since before the panicked call. Since before the bolt to the airport. Since before the relieving (yes) and infuriating (for sure) hospital visit. Since before the white-knuckle flight home. Since before the death-defying taxi ride back to the sanctum that is my home.

I grabbed a carrot and then...

This was not the first time I've aspirated/choked/or whatever the correct medical term would be on something–far, far from the first time. I've almost choked to death on—among other things—a taco chip, a piece of chicken, a bean in a three-bean salad and a poppy seed. You heard me, a poppy seed.

Like I said, there just might be something wrong with my throat.

Each of these times, while I was struggling to breathe, trying to Heimlich myself by mashing my ribcage against a dining room chair (too high) or the office chair (too narrow, too hard) and punching myself in the sternum (not painful enough followed by too painful), I was thinking, *Oh, so this is it. This is when I will die.*

Maybe I should have been sitting down. Maybe I was eating too fast. Maybe it was too big a bite. Maybe I should have been drinking water. Maybe you're supposed to angle your food in just the right way. Maybe my whole body was constricted, including my throat that I might have something wrong with anyway.

This is it! This is when I will die.

How interminable that moment was. Long enough to spin out what seemed the inevitable outcome: I will die and no one will discover me until the smell permeates the hall and my pets have, well, you know. Long enough to berate myself for my long-standing habit of not slowing down and not being more mindful. Long enough to be suspended in a moment of knowing just how very, completely and utterly un-ready I was.

5

TERROR MANAGEMENT THEORY

You can imagine how excited I was to come across this. Most definitely, yes please, for sure. You must have been thinking of me when you devised this theory. Not an iota of doubt that I need help managing my terror. And, P.S., I also need help managing the way I think about my terror, which can feel so idiosyncratic, sissified, and narcissistic compared to people who, at least on the surface, seem so cavalier and equanimous about their own mortality. Maybe I'm not alone in this. Or maybe it's my age. Or maybe, of course, it could be just me.

Heading to the library.

But first, some background.

In 1902, William James published *The Varieties of Religious Experience*. He writes, "Back of everything is the great spectre [sic] of universal death, the all-encompassing blackness...We need a life not correlated with death... a kind of good that will not perish, a good in fact that flies beyond the Goods of nature. And so with most of us:... a little irritable weakness... will bring the worm at the core of all of our usual springs of delight into full view, and turn us into melancholy metaphysicians."

Hold on. Come again?! Yowza!

The worm at the core. YES!

In 1974, the Pulitzer Prize for General Nonfiction was awarded to Ernest Becker's book *The Denial of Death*. Becker's big idea is that the majority of our actions are undertaken primarily as a means to ignore or evade (yeah, good luck with that!) death. He went so far as to suggest that our character itself is formed around the denial of our mortality. This defense, he asserts, is a necessary component of functioning in the world and also a character-armor that masks and obscures genuine self-knowledge. Becker writes, "...the idea of death, the fear of it, haunts the human animal like nothing else; it is a mainspring of human activity—activity designed largely to avoid the fatality of death, to overcome it by denying in some way that it is the final destiny for man."

And there's more. According to Becker, we transcend —or try to transcend—the dilemma of our mortality by focusing on our symbolic selves. He uses concepts he calls our *heroism project* or *immortality project*. By this, he means activities we engage in that make us feel relevant— things like having children, creating art, engaging in social activism, and other things like writing books (busted!). These grand-sounding concepts, he suggests, serve to imbue our lives with significance and obscure our experience of "self-negation." Oof! That's what I'm talking about, guys! Self-negation. How horrible is that notion!

The denial of death. At the center of it all.

Enter *The Worm at the Core*. In this 2015 book, Sheldon Solomon, Jeff Greenberg, and Tom Pyszczynski use James's evocative phrase and build on Becker's research to develop what they call Terror Management Theory (TMT).

Maybe you're like me. When I heard that title, I assumed that I'd be presented with a researched checklist of ways I could manage my terror. Step 1: breathe. Step 2: journal... Step 3: breathe some more ... all the way to Step 76: poof, all your fear is gone!

But nope, not the roadmap I was hoping for. That said, the book definitely does put flesh on the bone.

According to TMT, anxiety about death drives just about everything. These authors contend that we need to insulate ourselves from the deep fear that we may be living an insignificant life destined to be erased by death. Even more than that, though. They go on to contend that we adopt worldviews that protect our self-esteem and allow us to believe that we play an important role in a meaningful world. This, according to the TMT folks, is a way of assuring ourselves that we are part of an important group, which reinforces a sense of cultural significance and confirms our self-importance. If there is credence to this theory, I'm sure you can predict one giant downside: needing to feel a part of an important group can slip into a belief that the group with which one identifies is not just important, but superior to others. Drumroll: enter prejudice in all its ugly forms.

(I am a little confused, though, about how feeling relevant and important does much more that put a wisp-thin veil over the terror. Might help for a minute or two but....)

Now, you might ask—as I sure do—what to do with this terror? After all the research and theorizing—cogent and illuminating as it might be—what next? Yes, all these theories make sense. All the machinations and mind games and denial in service of keeping the wolf at bay. It all makes sense. What to do, though, when it's all laid bare?

What spoke to my head in reading these scholarly works did not reach down into my gut where the fear (read: terror) lives. Yes, this journey of mine is in a rather nascent stage. My earnest, deliberate search for more equanimity is quite fresh. One thing I do believe, though: when there is more congruity between this head and this gut of mine, I know I will have made some progress in the terror-management department.

6

STEALING FROM MAGGIE SMITH

If you haven't read Maggie Smith's luminous memoir, *You Could Make This Place Beautiful,* I suggest you stop reading this right now and head out to your local library or bookstore tout de suite!

I'll wait.

Ok, now that you've read Smith's memoir, you know that she begins several chapters this way:

"A friend told me that every book starts with an unanswerable question. Then what is mine?"

Which had me wondering, yeah, what exactly is *my* unanswerable question?

And does it have to be just one question because, as it turns out, I have several. Like off the top of my head I wonder:

Will I ever be less afraid of dying?

Or

How can I get more comfortable with my mortality?

Or

Am I the only one who feels this much fear?

Or

Will my unabsolved sins and misdeeds doom me for

eternity and what if karma is a real thing and I have to come back as a slug or if there really is a place called Hell and that's where I end up, what about that?

Or

Has my small life had any meaning?

Or

Will anyone miss me when I'm gone?

Or

How will people remember me, assuming they do remember me, and what will they say about me, assuming they say anything?

Or

Is there any slim, microscopic chance that my consciousness will live on after I die?

Or

What if I am terrified at the end and the Buddhists are right that one's emotional state at the moment of death has a profound effect on their afterlife and karma and the path to enlightenment and that no matter how hard I try I will be a grasping, bullheaded, terrified mess of a never-reaching-enlightenment cry baby? Talk about pressure!

Or

Will I be able to contact my loved ones after I die? Or see what happens in their lives?

Or

What if there really is a God and I will be punished for all my blasphemy?

Or

Will there be any Liz-ness after I die or will that just be the end of it?

And if you give me time, I'm sure I could think of even more.

7

REGRETS, I'VE HAD A FEW

Sometimes I wonder if this is the problem, this whole thing about regrets. Could it be that those annoying people who have lived their lives with no look-back at all the things they wished they'd done differently, could it be that those are the people who think, "Death? Sure, no biggie." ?

In a 2015 interview on *Fresh Air* with Terry Gross, Toni Morrison had this to say about what it's like to think back on herself as a mother when she was raising her children: "Now that I'm 84, I remember everything as a mistake, and I regret everything."

Me too, Toni. I regret everything.

Of course I'm being hyperbolic. No, I do not actually regret everything. Things I do not regret: I do not regret my mis-spent and utterly unserious youth. Amazingly and maybe hard to believe, I also don't regret my poor and misguided romantic relationship decisions. I do not regret oafish interactions with friends and colleagues borne out of unconsciousness. I don't regret my parenting in the last couple of decades.

It's about my first years as a mother. Of course, I'm

betting that most mothers look back and wish they'd known then what they know now; who cringe/worry/obsess about some of the decisions/actions/attitudes they took as they were raising their kids; who think/believe/worry that the issues/struggles/challenges their adult kids face would be fewer/inconsequential/painless had they been (and I'm talking about myself here) a better/more mature/less self-centered/more psychologically developed/more complete mother.

For those of you who don't look back like that, props to you. You're a better man than I am, Gunga Din. But I sure do. My glib excuse/explanation/justification is that a) I was so young, both chronologically and psychologically and, b) believe it or not, those were the days before "parenting" was even a word. Scratch that last sentence, please. That's most definitely glib. The candid and embarrassing truth is that when my children were young I was stressed, impatient and unhappy. I was self-centered and callow. And I'm not even sure I had what other people think of as a natural mothering instinct, never having had a great role model myself for one thing. Also—and this is hard to admit–I was mostly interested in my own needs in whatever present moment I was in. I came by this naturally. It was, in fact, my birthright. When I was growing up, there was zero discussion of values. There was no modeling of service or empathy or charity. Self-focus in the extreme was the unarticulated but blatant value.

If I did have any parenting philosophy it would be that I wanted my kids to be independent because–and at the time the antecedents for this motivation were somewhat opaque to me–independence is what propelled me out of a dysfunctional family. But my laser focus on independence meant the emotional needs of my children were often back-seated in my mind, not in a way that was conscious and transparent to me but back-seated nonetheless.

I am so very sorry, dear girls. Please know how fervently I wish I could go back with today's mind.

And just to complicate and maybe normalize my angst about my mothering at least a little bit, there is a real and well-documented phenomenon called *fetal-maternal microchimerism*. It seems that during pregnancy, fetal cells travel into the mother's bloodstream, even making their way into organs, tissues, and bones, remaining there for years and even decades. Decades! And there's research to show that these fetal cells aren't just passive guests. If a mother's heart is injured, for example, fetal cells have been found to migrate to the damaged area and transform into heart-specific cells to help repair the tissue. With this kind of maternal/child interplay, is it any wonder that mothers–that I–would worry and rehash parenting decisions, probably until the end of time?

Still—

Truth be told, I think if I had to identify what the most powerful driving force and motivation has been in my life for the last two or three decades it would be to try and make up for the regrets I carry about myself as a mother. No way am I implying perfection–I still make some dumbass decisions. But I am doing better, this I know. The thing is, I do not feel nearly done and I am positive that I will carry this same, exact motivation with me until I cash in my last chip.

Years ago I did a post-doc program in Gestalt therapy, a system with a foundational belief that people are best thought of as whole entities consisting of body, mind, and emotions. The Gestalt mantra is that the whole is greater than the sum of its parts. We learned about some super cool experiments of perception like the figure-ground pictures which I'm guessing you might remember–probably the most famous example being the one where you can toggle between seeing a vase in the middle and two profiles facing each other.

One of the principles that has really stuck with me from that program is the Gestalt principle of closure. This is a visual perception law that describes how people tend to fill in the gaps in an image to perceive a complete object. This is our brain's tendency to insert missing information and perceive incomplete shapes as complete, essentially closing the gaps to create a recognizable whole image, even when parts are missing. For example, here we see a panda, not just 5 black blobs.

I used to love studying these experiments and learning about all the ways our brains are wired to find closure.

Yes, but—

When I think about this closure thing, I wonder how it might be affecting my feelings about my death. Here's what I mean. Had I been the mother I wish I'd been, I probably/maybe wouldn't have this naggy feeling of incompleteness. If I didn't look back with regret, maybe I'd experience my life as more integrated and whole-a start to finish complete circle. And who knows, if I felt this kind of closure, maybe then I would be able to face my mortality with less fear.

As much and as earnestly as I try now to forestall or at least minimize any future regret, there is not a single, damn thing I can do about back then. Back then will always remain what it was: forever deficient, forever wanting, forever incomplete. So you can shove it, Gestalt theory, and your belief that we automatically complete this circle! I cannot imagine what it would take to close the circle of this life of mine. I just don't know how it's possible to feel the peace and release of closure when freeing myself of regret feels too much like letting myself off the hook which feels unfair to my children who deserved a more complete mother.

My heart aches for what is impossible to change.

8

THIS BODY OF MINE

After all these many years walking around in this body of mine, I am pretty well attached. Well acquainted, too. That hemangioma on the pinky finger of my left hand? I've had that for decades. By now, it's an old friend. The stupid scars on my right shin from the third-degree burns I stupidly got on a stupid all-day sailing trip in college, out in the blazing East Coast midsummer sun, stupidly slicked up with baby oil. Those ridiculous things that pass for toenails on my little toes. Not to mention all the changes: my once thin ankles that somehow got thicker—even if I haven't gained that much weight. The puppet lines on either side of my mouth. And the skin on my arms which—and please tell me how this happens overnight—has mysteriously and horrifyingly been replaced by my mother's.

Yup, I am attached to this body of mine.

The question is this: what should I do with this constant companion when I die? It's a question whose urgency only grows. I know that some people ask their kids for their input on the subject. But I know my kids. I'd hate to burden them with what they—I'm pretty sure—

would feel is an onerous decision, something they, I am convinced, would feel is not their decision to make.

So, I've been thinking a lot about it. What do I want to do with this body of mine when I die?

Let me tell you, I do not love the choices.

I've ruled out burial—at least the usual kind. So many reasons. Burial never really made much sense to me. Maybe in the days when generations of a family lived on and on in the same place—maybe on the family farm—and there was the romanticism of having a gravesite to visit on the anniversary of a loved one's death. It was a place to bring flowers, talk to the the headstone, see a name and honorifics carved in marble. Maybe have a picnic and tell stories.

That sounds sweet.

But there's so much wrong about it to me. For one thing, who knows if my descendants will continue to live wherever it would be that I'd be buried? Would they feel reluctant to move? Would they worry they'd be abandoning me if they did? And even if they don't move away, there's a kind of demand: aren't you going to visit Mom this week, this month, this year? Like, oh shit, we forgot to visit Mom on her birthday! That gravesite could taunt them, wagging a foam finger, laying a big guilt trip on them. Bad kids! Ingrates!

Regardless, there is the obscene—in my opinion—use of land. If there's enough land for a cemetery, how about using it to build a playground or a nature preserve, or a dog park—something we all could use, not just some tract of land reserved for a handful of dutiful or grieving or guilt-bound relatives.

Just in case, I should add this caveat: if you want to bury me at Père Lachaise, in that case I take it all back.

And embalming! Good God. How grotesque! Even with my deliberately limited knowledge of the process (I closed my eyes in every episode of *Six Feet Under* when David or Rico were embalming), just saying the word creates these unwelcome images that colonize my consciousness. And can't you just smell the formaldehyde? That smell has lived with me since sixth-grade biology when we dissected that unfortunate frog.

Embalming—grotesque and creepy and, to me, frankly bizarre. Maybe it's my Jewishness coming through, but if you really want to bury someone, just get it over with. Wrap the body in a plain shroud, put it in a pine box, and pop it into the ground ASAP. Sure, there's still the issue of how we use the limited resource of land—unless maybe you live in North Dakota with the other twelve people.

Also, let's talk about coffins. There must be a hefty dose of magical thinking that supports spending the money on what some of these elaborate coffins surely must cost. Yes, you can get one on the cheap for around a thousand bucks or—if you really love your mother—you can buy one in Promethean Bronze (??) for about $22K. Coffins of steel or bronze or copper or fiberglass are said to be more durable and weather-resistant, so they will better protect the body from the elements, which—what?? Exactly why do we believe we need to protect a corpse from the elements? Are we also outfitting the dead bodies in rain slickers and puffy coats?

True, these coffins look positively maggot-proof which, of course, is also magical thinking. Yeah, it might take months or years or decades, but those, too, will decompose. Even bodies mummified in ancient Egypt will eventually deteriorate beyond any recognition. Sure, it might take hundreds of years, but all bodies will eventually decompose and then—it's cue the maggots.

Laws vary by state, but there actually are an increasing number of natural burial grounds where you can plop a body straight in the dirt—maybe an essential oil solution as an alternative to formaldehyde. Or now there's what's called an infinity burial suit, a biodegradable outfit woven with a mix of mycelia and other microorganisms. As the body decomposes, fungi help with decomposition, neutralizing toxins in the body, and transferring nutrients back to the environment. But here's the thing: those fucking maggots again! So, nope.

Burial in any form = too dirty, too icky, too maggoty.

I always assumed I'd be cremated, mostly because it seemed like a binary choice: the ground or the incinerator. I have some of my mother's ashes in a minty-green Chinese ceramic apothecary jar. It sits on a bookshelf right next to the TV in my living room so she/it is in my view every day when I watch *Jeopardy!* And more times than not, when my eyes land on that jar, she passes through my consciousness. *Hi, Mom.* I am sure I think of her much more often than I would if that jar of her ashes were not something in my eyesight every day.

I also have some of my late husband's ashes in a ceramic pot on one of my bedside tables. It's an antique French honey pot with the word "Miel" on it, which I bought because we had planned to move to France before he got sick and because he once told me that no one had ever called him honey before. Maybe I think of him more frequently because he/it is something I see every day, multiple times. Maybe. Probably.

So I've thought that my kids might like that—having something tangible to keep my memory alive. On the other hand, knowing them, they might find it a bit macabre to keep a jar of my pulverized bones on a bookcase. And yes, I have asked them about this and here's what they said: "LALALALALALA!"

Sidebar: I've wondered if the ashes I have are even the actual ashes of my mother or my husband. Maybe they were just swept up at the end of the day on the floor of the crematorium. A mix of all the people incinerated that day. Or if they are even human ashes. My dear, late friend —someone who had the most delicious sense of nonconformity and twisted sense of humor—was kind of officiating a funeral service and had somehow lost the ashes of the deceased (!!) so she filled a container with kitty litter. No one knew the difference. I'm just saying.

And another thing: this is something that hadn't crossed my mind until a friend told me she felt uncomfortable about "separating" her mother. You know, like some of her ashes get divided between her and her brothers; some get spread at her favorite spot on the coast; and some taken to Scotland where her ancestors are. Dividing her mother up like that felt, well, kind of icky. And yeah, now that I think about it, I can see why.

Truth is, I've been souring on cremation anyway, a turn that started with the funeral people zipping my husband into a heavy black plastic bag, loading him in a hearse, taking him away to be stored in a refrigerated drawer until the morning shift arrived and there was room in the oven.

Another picture that I wish I could expunge.

And there's also the fact that cremation creates toxic

air pollutants like nitrogen oxides and carbon monoxide —there's that too.

Besides, cremation is so permanent!

Also, I'm a Jew, so ovens.

Aha—what about being the best human citizen, one of the noble ones who donate their bodies to science and play some role in a cure that millions have been waiting for? To be a note in that symphony! That sounds a little bit not so horrible.

I read about how this process goes at Cambridge University in England. To start, they do not use the word "cadaver." It's "donor" or "subject" to be as respectful as possible. At the end of the academic year, the medical students take part in a committal service when they learn the names of the people they've worked on. It sounds like a very emotionally laden service where the students come to know the donors as they were in life. The committal service is a time for all involved to pay their respects to the donors. Each table group writes a tribute to their donor, and these tributes can then be given to the donors' relatives. This is followed by another service which includes the relatives of the deceased.

Not sure this is how medical schools in the United States do it—hopefully so, but I've read some truly mind-bendingly awful things. For example, there is, apparently, this whole industry of body donation. A relative may believe that they are donating to an institute where the respect shown at Cambridge will be what their loved one receives, but *caveat venditor*, man.

In one of the pages and pages of accounts I read and wish I hadn't, a woman donated her husband's body to the Biological Resource Center in Phoenix, Arizona, assuming, I bet, that she would be contributing to a good cause. What happened next was that his remains were sent to the Department of Defense where "he" was used as a crash test dummy in a simulated Humvee explosion. Horrifying!

FutureGenex, a company in Washington State that facilitated what is called whole body donations, was found guilty of dumping body parts in a remote Arizona forest. Damn! Other companies sell various body parts to various recipients: $500 for a head, $250 for a foot, $300 for a cervical spine. The mind boggles, wondering why someone wants to buy a dead person's foot. Yeah, I know, there's a fetish for everything but oh my good God!

When the FBI raided one such warehouse, they found conditions of the donors' remains so abhorrent that the agents required trauma therapy due to the disturbing, graphic scenes they encountered.

(By the way, just so this doesn't discourage anyone from being an organ donor, this whole body donation horror is a whole other kettle o' fish.)

And then there is Cryogenics or Cryonics. At Alcor Life Extension in Phoenix, Arizona, for somewhere between $17–$100 per month you can purchase a membership. But wait! The membership itself does not cover the process of freezing and thawing. (I know!) For that, most people buy a whole life insurance policy which would cover the multiple hundreds of thousands of dollars which is the cost for the actual process—unless, of course, you just want to freeze your brain—known as neuropreservation. For that, a policy of somewhere around $100K would suffice.

And please, someone: tell me the reasoning behind freezing your brain. That's some other level sci-fi shit, if you ask me.

This whole freezing process—whole body or not—needs to start immediately after a person is pronounced dead. At that point, a team member swoops in, gets the body to Arizona, and begins a process of first perfusion (which means infusing the body with cryoprotectants, whatever in the sam hill that is), and then the "patient" (i.e., dead person) is cooled to -196C. 'Nough said!

We've all heard the rumors that Walt Disney had himself frozen and some say his body is buried under Cinderella's Castle in Anaheim. Blah, blah, blah, and probably total bullshit. But Walt Disney aside, currently there are about 500 people who have had themselves cryonically preserved in the world. There are more than 300 in cryosleep in the US, 50 people in Russia, around 100 in Europe, and more than 30 pets in Arizona. (For a fiction writer's take on this option, I point you to *Zero K* by Don DeLillo.)

Maybe I'll be proven wrong about this cryo-thing. Then again, I'm skeptical that were I to be brought back to life in 100 years, I would find a world I'd actually want to live in. Also, I wouldn't know a single soul, so that would suck, since I'm not great at meeting new people already.

Bottom line, those hucksters ain't getting my money.

And now to the most creepy, most maggoty, and most definitely-not option for me: the body farm. These deceptively pastoral-sounding (a.k.a. science-fiction-movie-title) facilities were the brainchild of Dr. William Bass, who, in 1972, founded the first such, um, facility at University of Tennessee. What happens is that corpses are left out in the elements to see what happens when the body decomposes. You can look it up for yourself if you are interested, but if I explain what happens over days and weeks and months, I might just hurl. Suffice to say, the intention here is to train law enforcement officers in recovering human remains in crime scenes and determining the time and cause of death. Okay, I guess I see the utility of that, but for me?

HARDEST POSSIBLE NO!

Here's another option: aquamation, a.k.a. alkaline hydrolysis. When I first heard about this, I had visions of sailors returning their fallen comrades to the sea, or pirates walking someone off the plank. All natural, for sure. No chemicals, no storing a body in anything for any amount of time. Just dump me in the ocean and I'm instantly fish food and part of the earth's ecosystem. Turns out that's not quite how it goes. The body is placed in a vessel of water and alkali and heated to temperatures between 200–300 degrees F and, after some amount of time, only bones are left, which are then processed into a powder = the remains = the fish food.

Maybe.

Or how about this? There are some companies who can take carbon from your cremated remains, subject this to high-pressure and high-temperature technology, and voila! A diamond. You can choose your cut and style, wear it as a ring, a pendant, or whatever. But again, I cannot imagine a world in which my family would want to walk around wearing my ashes at a cocktail party.

But wait, there's more. You can turn your body into fireworks... or a playable vinyl record... or a glass sculpture... or you can float into heaven in a balloon... or get launched into outer space.

Oh, human ingenuity!

I'm zeroing in on what so far is the least creepy, least disgusting, least toxic, least maggoty option: human composting. There is a company in Washington State that describes their process of soil transformation as a natural, environmentally friendly alternative to burial or cremation. I'm a little worried that if I do too deep a dive into the how of it all I may recoil, but the elevator pitch goes like this: their process recreates systems found in the natural world so that organically occurring microbes break the body down on a molecular level, producing nutrient-rich soil. Again, I don't want to think about it too much because how a body would turn into soil naturally is a bit of a mystery to me but I might just decide to take their word for it. Families can choose how much soil they would like returned to them, and the rest is sent to a conservation site on the Olympic Peninsula.

Right now, I'm thinking it's that option. Either that, or not die.

Update: Since I didn't want to wait too long—and let's face it, I ain't getting any younger—I took a virtual tour of the turn-me-into-dirt-and-add-me-to-the-Olympic-Peninsula company. They showed me the stainless steel vessels in which my body would be placed upon my death. Besides me, only some organic mulch and wood chips and the my own microbes would be in that vessel. No chemicals, no insects. The process, I'm told, mimics what would happen in nature.

I know, you might be thinking what I'm thinking: what if in the next few years some amazing, unforeseen option suddenly appears, in which case, oh well, live and learn; die and it won't matter anyway.

Update #2: You can find me one day as you wander the Olympic Peninsula.

9

ST. JOSEPH, MY MAN

It turns out that St. Joseph has several badges on his lapel. Of course there is the biggie: Head of the Holy Family, a silent but loyal husband to Mary, and father–or should I say, step-father– to Jesus to whom he taught carpentry and faithfulness to the Torah.

It's hard to top that one, sure, but Pope Pius IX declared him to be patron and protector of the Catholic Church. But wait, there's more. He's also patron saint of virgins; of the Universal Church; of families, fathers, expectant mothers; of travelers and immigrants; of house sellers and buyers; of craftsmen and engineers; of social justice; and of working people. Where did he find the time!

For my purposes, though, it was learning that St. Joseph was also known as the *Patron of a Happy Death*. Gotta say, when I first came across this I thought it might be a parody–a *Saturday Night Live* skit or an *Onion* headline. But no. The term "happy," in this context, does not connote the emotion of being glad or cheerful or giggly. Instead, this "happy" is about being peaceful, full of faith and hope in Jesus Christ. And this kind of happy is believed to carry with it a certain kind of joy. For believers, since we all will eventually face death, each one of us needs and wants the help of St. Joseph, a loving spiritual father, as we all are on the road of passing from this life to the next.

It seems that Joseph was anointed with this moniker because, it is believed, he died while he was comforted by the loving presence of Jesus and Mary. This, for him, was *a happy death.*

A happy death is just not a concept I can ever imagine getting behind. But maybe this is a case of "lost in translation." Maybe, instead of "happy," how about peaceful? As I researched St. Joseph, that's the word that kept coming up for me. Afterall, nowhere is he described as grinning, cracking up, or telling jokes (did they even tell jokes in biblical times?). Instead, what I have read about his death—though, of course, who can really know?—is that he was comforted by the loving presence of his family; that he had atoned and said his final good-byes.

Okay, now we're talking. This I can get behind.

St. Joseph: If you will listen to a heathen. Let me be lucky enough to have apologized where needed; to forgive anything that isn't unforgivable; to have left nothing unsaid; and mostly, to be surrounded by my cherished family. That, for sure, would be as close to happy as I could get.

10

DON'T FORGET ME

It used to really get under my skin–really bug the shit out of me– when my mother would say, and I mean repeatedly she would say, *'Don't forget me.'* I mean how *could* I and even if I could, of course, why *would* I, even with everything, why would I? And what did she mean anyway?

It always felt to me like yet another narcissistic iteration, like another of her embarrassing outbursts leveled at some dumbfounded clerk only trying to do their job: *Do you know who I am?* Which, of course, no. No, they did not know who she was.

This among the very many ways she had to keep herself in the center of our consciousness all the damn time.

Sorry, mom. Another apology. Now I get it. Maybe it's because, like her, I have an over-inflated sense of my own importance. Shudder the thought. Or, the exact opposite which, by the way, is actually what underlies much of what we experience as inflated ego. That is, what we see as arrogance is often compensation for a sense of worthlessness.

Or, maybe it's that we all strive for a significance that belies our tiny blip of existence. Maybe it's how terrifying it is to know how forgettable we all will be in the long run. Because unless you are Jonas Salk or Mickey Mantle, in some amount of time–a hundred years, two hundred? Not a soul will remember you ever existed.

Whatever underlies the need, I feel it: Don't forget me.

11

DEATH ATTITUDE PROFILE, REVISED

Death Attitude Profile-Revised (DAP-R)

Wong, P.T.P., Reker, G.T., & Gesser, G.

This questionnaire contains a number of statements related to different attitudes toward death. Read each statement carefully, and then decide the extent to which you agree or disagree. For example, an item might read: "Death is a friend." Indicate how well you agree or disagree by circling one of the following: **SA** = strongly agree; **A** = agree; **MA** = moderately agree; **U** = undecided; **MD** = moderately disagree; **D** = disagree; **SD** = strongly disagree. Note that the scales run both from *strongly agree* to *strongly disagree* and from *strongly disagree* to *strongly agree*.

If you strongly agreed with the statement, you would circle **SA**. If you strongly disagreed you would circle **SD**. If you are undecided, circle **U**. However, try to use the undecided category sparingly.

It is important that you work through the statements and answer each one. Many of the statements will seem alike, but all are necessary to show slight differences in attitudes.

1. Death is no doubt a grim experience.   SD   D   MD   U   MA   (A)   (SA)

2. The prospects of my own death arouses anxiety in me.   (SA)   A   MA   U   MD   D   SD

3. I avoid death thoughts at all costs.   SA   (A)   MA   U   MD   D   SD

4. I believe that I will be in heaven after I die.   (SD)   D   MD   (U)   MA   A   SA

5. Death will bring an end to all my troubles.   SD   D   MD   U   MA   (A)   (SA)

6. Death should be viewed as a natural, undeniable, and unavoidable event.   SA   A   (MA)   U   MD   D   SD

7. I am disturbed by the finality of death.   (SA)   A   MA   U   MD   D   SD

8. Death is an entrance to a place of ultimate satisfaction.   SD D MD U MA A SA

9. Death provides an escape from this terrible world.   SA A MA U MD D SD

10. Whenever the thought of death enters my mind, I try to push it away.   SD D MD U MA A SA

11. Death is deliverance from pain and suffering.   SD D MD U MA A SA

12. I always try not to think about death.   SA A MA U MD D SD

13. I believe that heaven will be a much better place than this world.   SA A MA U MD D SD

14. Death is a natural aspect of life.   SA A MA U MD D SD

15. Death is a union with God and eternal bliss.   SD D MD U MA A SA

16. Death brings a promise of a new and glorious life.   SA A MA U MD D SD

17. I would neither fear death nor welcome it.   SA A MA U MD D SD

18. I have an intense fear of death.   SD D MD U MA A SA

19. I avoid thinking about death altogether.   SD D MD U MA A SA

20. The subject of life after death troubles me greatly.   SA A MA U MD D SD

21. The fact that death will mean the end of everything as I know it frightens me. **(SA)** A MA U MD D SD

22. I look forward to a reunion with my loved ones after I die. **(SD)** D MA U MA A SA

23. I view death as a relief from earthly suffering. SA A MA U MD **(D)** SD

24. Death is simply a part of the process of life. SA **(A)** MA U MD D SD

25. I see death as a passage to an eternal and blessed place. SA A MA U **(MD)** **(D)** SD

26. I try to have nothing to do with the subject of death. **(SD)** D MD U MA A SA

27. Death offers a wonderful release of the soul. SD D MD **(U)** **(MA)** A SA

28. One thing that gives me comfort in facing death is my belief in the afterlife. SD **(D)** MD U MA A SA

29. I see death as a relief from the burden of this life. **(SD)** D MD U MA A SA

30. Death is neither good nor bad. SA A MA U **(MD)** D SD

31. I look forward to life after death. SA A MA U MD D **(SD)**

32. The uncertainty of not knowing what happens after death worries me. SD D MD U MA A **(SA)**

Scoring Key for the Death Attitude Profile-Revised (DAP-R)

Items

- Fear of Death (7 items)1,2,7,18,20,21,32
- Death Avoidance (5 items)3,10,12,19,26
- Neutral Acceptance (5 items)6,14,17,24,30

- Approach Acceptance (10 items)4,8,13,15,16,22,25,27,28,31
- Escape Acceptance (5 items)5,9,11,23,29

Scores for all items are from 1 to 7 in the direction of strongly disagree (1) to strongly agree (7). For each dimension, a mean scale score can be computed by dividing the total scale score by the number of items forming each scale.

So, my results are:

- Fear of Death: (negative thoughts and feelings about death) 5.4
- Death Avoidance: (efforts to avoid thinking about death) 2.6
- Neutral Acceptance: (acceptance of death as natural, neither feared nor welcomed) 4.4
- Approach Acceptance: (view of death as an entrance to a better afterlife) 3.1
- Escape Acceptance: (death as seen as a relief from suffering) 3

I honestly don't understand the usefulness of this questionnaire. You could have just asked me and I would have told you that numero uno for me is *negative thoughts and feelings about death.* That said, color me surprised to see that my next highest score is *neutral acceptance.* Maybe I was too hasty when I took this questionnaire. Or maybe my unconscious knows more than I do. Maybe what I have considered a wholesale fear and lack of acceptance of my ultimate demise is actually more nuanced than that. Whatever my level of apprehension (how mild that word is!), of course…death is inevitable, death is natural. *Neither feared nor welcomed?* Not so sure about that one.

12

READING DYLAN THOMAS

Do not go gentle into that good night,
Old age should burn and rave at close of day;
Rage, rage against the dying of the light.
Though wise men at their end know dark is right,
Because their words had forked no lightning they
Do not go gentle into that good night.
Good men, the last wave by, crying how bright
Their frail deeds might have danced in a green bay,
Rage, rage against the dying of the light.
Wild men who caught and sang the sun in flight,
And learn, too late, they grieved it on its way,
Do not go gentle into that good night.

Grave men, near death, who see with blinding sight
Blind eyes could blaze like meteors and be gay,
Rage, rage against the dying of the light.
And you, my father, there on the sad height,
Curse, bless, me now with your fierce tears, I pray.
Do not go gentle into that good night.
Rage, rage against the dying of the light.

Reading Dylan Thomas

Do not go gentle into that good night, — *what's so good about it?*

Old age should burn and rave at close of day; — *yup!*

Rage, rage against the dying of the light.

Though wise men at their end know dark is right, — *I get how wise men know it's inevitable, but right?*

Because their words had forked no lightning they

Do not go gentle into that good night.

Good men, the last wave by, crying how bright

Their frail deeds might have danced in a green bay, — *maybe if I'd had more impact??*

Rage, rage against the dying of the light.

Wild men who caught and sang the sun in flight, } *blissful ignorance?*

And learn, too late, they grieved it on its way, *but why "too late"?*

Do not go gentle into that ~~good night.~~ *? again?*

Grave men, near death, who see with blinding sight

Blind eyes could blaze like meteors and be gay, *So, are those who are blind to death happier?*

Rage, rage against the dying of the light.

And you, my father, there on the sad height, = *The end?*

yes.

? (Curse, bless) me now with your fierce tears, I pray.

Do not go gentle into that good night. } *I am raging but*

Rage, rage against the dying of the light. } *some "gentle-ness" seems nice*

13

LIVING LIKE EMILY

If I Can Stop One Heart From Breaking

If I can stop one heart from breaking,
I shall not live in vain;
If I can ease one life the aching,
Or cool one pain,
Or help one fainting robin
Unto his nest again,
I shall not live in vain.

—Emily Dickinson

Which brings me to the topic of *meaning*. This month I re-read *Man's Search for Meaning*, Viktor Frankl's vital memoir schooling us in the power and importance of living a life of meaning even in the most seemingly meaningless of circumstances. After his liberation from Auschwitz, Frankl–a psychiatrist and philosopher–developed a therapeutic approach he called *Logotherapy* which was aimed at helping his patients find meaning in their lives.

Logotherapy is based on Søren Kierkegaard's work, especially his focus on one's existential *Will to Meaning*, specifically on the importance of us finding the *individual* meaning of our own lives, our own particular motivation for getting out of bed in the morning. In his 1835 journal Kierkegaard writes, "What I really need is to get clear about what I must do, not what I must know, except insofar as knowledge must precede every act... [T]he crucial thing is to find a truth which is truth for me, to find the idea for which I am willing to live and die."

This way of philosophizing about meaning is opposed to the Nietzschean doctrine that the *Will to Power* is our main motivating force. In this context, *power* is primarily about self-affirmation and overcoming limitations, though reading up on this theory, there is not much flesh on the bone. In some places he talks about *personal power* but there is also reference to *power over others*. That said, Nietzsche was quite firmly planted in his theory, saying: "This world is the will to power—and nothing besides! And you yourselves are also this will to power—and nothing besides!"

Logotherapy and its concept of what gives us meaning is also quite different from the way Freud saw it. For Freud, it's all about the *Pleasure Principle*, the theory that human behavior is primarily and at root motivated by seeking pleasure and avoiding pain. In this theory, pleasure and avoidance of pain is related to the *id* and is a hallmark of infancy and early childhood. The idea is that people are, by and large, motivated by a desire to satisfy their needs and avoid unpleasant experiences.

Whatever the theoretical orientation, I have started to wonder about how the concept of meaning might be affecting my feelings about my ever-nearing death. I can definitely get on board with Nietzsche if his *Will to Power* is about *personal power* which, sure, is important to me. I want to feel agency and determination, yes. And duh, of course, I can jibe with Freud in that I want to maximize pleasure and minimize pain. Who doesn't? (Masochists excepted).

But whatever the theoretical orientation, the concept of meaning strikes a booming chord for me when I think about what might contribute to a more equanimous emotional state about my own mortality.

This is what I wonder: is there something about meaning or not enough meaning or not the right kind of meaning that I need to be focusing on? And maybe if I futz around with this whole meaning thing, it will shift my relationship to my mortality. Maybe finding deep meaning leads to satisfaction which leads to inner peace which leads to, hmmm, let's say equanimity which leads to transcendence which leads to *I'm going to die, no biggie*!

I gotta say, I have always been flummoxed by people who seem (emphasis on *seem*) so equanimous, so nonchalant, so unfazed about the incontrovertible fact that one day they will die. People! Have you really faced it, looked it square in the face? You will cease to exist! Cease! To! Exist! To be fair, it's only been in the last few years as time has marched me inexorably toward extinction that I have been on this quest of facing my mortality with more grace than I currently think I have.

If it is, indeed, meaning that leads to equanimity, then I may just need something more or different, meaning-wise. It's a bit of a mind-fuck when I start examining this concept of meaning in my own life, though. I have a family I love and help as much as they will allow. I have a community I am a part of, even if I typically scour around for any excuse to *not* leave my house. I have work which is undoubtedly meaningful. Over my decades as a psychologist I have worked with thousands of people and absolutely know that sometimes I am helpful. Every morning I buy a coffee for Daniel who sells the *Street Roots* paper.

In other words, my life has a kind of one-person-at-a-time meaning à la Emily Dickinson.

I'm just confused as to whether or not this meets Frankl's definition of a meaningful life. It's for sure not as meaningful as his was. He's in some rarified company, after all. In a hundred years, two hundred years, a century, probably for as long as humans will live on planet Earth and even beyond, people will be inspired by Frankl and in less than a hundred years, not a soul will know I ever existed. Frankl's life and work will live on until humans perish from the universe. That's some high octane meaning, man!

And what about someone like the late Jimmy Carter? People will read about Jimmy Carter who was President of the United States and then built a zillion low-income homes with his own frickin' bare hands and, oh yeah, cured guinea worm in Africa. The scope of it all. Some people live such big lives! Capital M meaning to my lower case. Is this what Frankl meant by a life of meaning? Does a life of lower case meaning count? Does the fact that I might have a positive impact on some individual people here and there really equate to those exalted souls whose impact is so broad and profound?

Of course it doesn't equate, but what I mean is this: *is it enough*? My efforts at leaving the world a better place—my stab at *tikkum olam*—they just seem like spit in the wind and, I am betting (read: fearing), not enough to venture fearlessly into the void if meaning is what is required. The thing is, I am not convinced that meaning or no meaning or big meaning or small meaning actually matter beyond our own earthly sense of satisfaction. Or a more base interpretation, if meaning matters beyond our own ego gratification.

My daughter recently asked me if I believed that the universe is benevolent. It would be so lovely to say yes, yes I do. Yes, I believe that the awesome forces which we do not have the capacity to understand are evidence of a loving God/force who/which would never banish us to senseless extinction. So lovely if I could get there. But leaving aside the sliver of my mind that can fully acknowledge all that is unknowable, I confess: I believe that we all are mucking around in an effort to make meaning of what is meaningless. We are here in an indifferent universe for a mere blip. All the sturm und drang, the big lives and the not-so-big, all of it gone in a nanosecond. No one is protected from death by accomplishment or fame or a life of meaning. Meaning or no meaning. Does it even matter?

I tend to groove with Camus' way of thinking about this all: "The absurdity arises when the human being seeks meaning in an indifferent universe...I continue to believe that this world has no ultimate meaning. But I know that something in it has a meaning and that is man, because he is the only creature to insist on having one."

Absurdism: how we live in a universe devoid of meaning and yet seek a life of meaning and purpose.

Are you depressed yet? True, I may be Exhibit A for what Frankl called the "existential vacuum," i.e. the belief that life is basically meaningless. But nothing so far has convinced me that all the scurrying around that we do to create meaning is much more than a mostly unconscious hedge against mortality. *If I do enough of the right kind of good deeds, then I won't die.* Emphasis here on the word *unconscious*. I doubt you'd find anyone who would, with a straight face, argue that because they started this charity or cured that disease or fostered hundreds of stray dogs, that they were awarded immortality, not that it isn't worthwhile to love and to help and to contribute. Especially about the dogs. All good and noble in this fleeting moment.

But when all's told? Me? I am inclined to cue Peggy Lee.

14

MANEKI-NEKO

My daughter brought me back a Maneki-neko from her trip to Japan. Maybe you have one too. It's the little waving cat figurine that you'll see in so many dry cleaners, nail salons, pachinko parlors, and restaurants, even outside Asia.

Maneki-neko literally means "beckoning cat" and these figurines are believed to bring good luck to the owner. It seems they are also feng shui items that need to be situated in the right place in the home or business to maximize their lucky powers. Ideally you should place this lucky cat in the south-eastern corner of a room to maximize whatever power they have to deliver such good fortune and wealth your way.

I hadn't read this placement advice when I put my little three inch figurine on the shelf in the living room where it faces me for most hours of every day. Lucky me, this just happens to be in the south-eastern corner.

So who knows, maybe tomorrow 1-7-12-25-18-31 will be the Powerball numbers.

But more to the point is this: I don't know if they all are solar powered but mine is. It waves non-stop, 24/7, with a little clicking sound. All day. This clicking sound. This perpetually waving cat seems to be reminding me:

>TICK
>TICK
>TICK
>TICK

All day, every day.

That frickin' cat. Taunting me. Like I could forget for even a nano-second:

>TICK
>TICK
>TICK
>TICK

Yeah, I Get It! Tick Fucking Tick, You Fucking Cat!

15

MEDIUMS & PSYCHICS & CHANNELERS, OH MY!

Many years ago, when my kids were in their single digits, I went to see a psychic. I have no recollection of why I went that first time, what it was that prompted me. Who knows. Might have just been curiosity. Or maybe some big change in my life. I've had more than my fair share of transitions so maybe that was the motivation. For years I didn't give that reading a second thought but about ten years later, details that were eerily prescient came flooding back.

The psychic had told me–not asked me, mind you..*told me*–she told me that my daughter–then in middle school–was a dancer. I said, no, she's not a dancer, she's never taken a dance class. She is a swimmer and a gymnast but no, she's definitely not a dancer. And the psychic said, no, she's a dancer. That was enough to leave me with a hefty dose of eye-roll.

I didn't bother telling my daughter about the misguided psychic and forgot about the whole experience until the second semester of her freshman year of college when she announced that she would be majoring in dance. And, cut to the chase, dance has been perhaps the most central and enduring focus of her life ever since.

Weird, huh.

That experience definitely made an impression, not enough to move me into the column of true believer but it did scooch me from strident cynic to somewhat persuadable skeptic.

Over the years I have visited psychics a few times. I've had my Akashic record uncovered, though gotta admit that experience was beyond puzzling. For one thing, nothing made sense and not a single thing seemed at all relevant and, more to the point, the whole concept was frankly unbelievable to me–no offense. But the foundational theory that there exists a "record" of all events, thoughts, emotions, and intentions that exist(ed) in the past, present and future, well, I may be an outlier but that's a road I'm disinclined to travel down in the future.

I've had my horoscope read maybe a dozen times and I am sure there will be more readings in my future. Frankly, because it's fun. And, after all, how many times in life do you have someone talk about YOU for a full hour straight? Almost every time I find the experience interesting, and then interesting, and then I have no idea what you're talking about. Often I end up feeling the way I do when I try to speak French with a native speaker. I understand maybe 4 out of 10 words, nod my head like it's all making sense and finally feel my eyes glaze over and it all just begins to sound like random words. *Your planets are ascending, there is a trine in the third house and there is a Saturn square Venus in Mid-May with Jupiter rising.* At which point I wish I had a translation app on my phone. I just want to cut to the chase and say *O—kay, but will my book get published?* Or, *What numbers should I play on the power ball?* Or, *Will I meet a dark, handsome stranger?*

All of this is true but what's also true is that I've watched all the shows on Netflix about mediums and psychics and near-death experiences and magicians and no one can tell me that David Blaine is not some sort of supernatural dude. (Have you seen the YouTube video of him with Harrison Ford? Hard to watch that and not be at least convincible that there is something beyond my puny understanding.)

But, but, but...it seems that any time I've watched a psychic work it starts like this: "I'm picking up the letter R, does the letter R mean something to anyone here? R? Or maybe it's J? James? John?" I mean, come on! I'm not exactly mocking, well maybe that's part of it. At the same time, I understand the power of projection. I understand the need to find peace. I understand the vulnerability and disorientation that invariably follows the loss of someone you dearly love. Been there, I truly get it. If your recently deceased husband's name was John and the psychic lady says she's channeling someone with a J name, well, of course you'd sit up in your seat. I would. Of course you'd suspend whatever disbelief you came in with. I would. Of course you'd be inclined to bestow the halo effect simply because of the letter J. I definitely would.

My mind is not super glued shut and it had been a few years since I'd visited this corner of the world and I started to wonder if a journey to the land of the occult might actually help me with my mortality terror. Specifically, I thought that if a medium could convince me that s/he could contact any of my deceased family or friends, then I might consider the possibility that there is more to follow this earthly existence.

I haven't really pulled on that thread though. Exactly what might it mean that there is more to follow? What would that look like? Yes, I have a vague sense that I would derive some amount of comfort from that, from the idea that it's not simply lights out. But if I give it even a cursory examination, I throw up my hands. When I try to fill in that picture, well, it's just so abstruse and hazy and vaguely theoretical that I'd rather watch TV.

Even so. I am genuinely aware that I don't know what I don't know. And people I am close to and trust have had very meaningful experiences. Plus, I cannot think of one single thing I have to lose. SO.....

Let the search for a medium begin.

Where I always start when looking for a recommendation for a dentist or a plumber or a CPA or a psychic is to ask friends and, no surprise, given we are citizens of the hipster heaven demi-monde that is Portland, Oregon, one of my friends had recently had an experience with a medium. The story she related pushed me back a skosh into the camp of scoffers.

Here's what she told me. My friend (I'll call her Jane) had enlisted the help of a medium in the hopes that she could make contact with her beloved mother who had recently died. It went something like this:

Jane: I want to contact my mother.

(Psychic closes her eyes and silently nods her head)

Psychic: She's coming through now, hold on.

(More silent eyes-closed-head-nodding)

Psychic: I see her. She is a very tall woman.

Jane: Umm, no she was actually quite short.

Psychic: Oh, I see. Hold on. (Silent-eyes-closed-head-nodding). Oh, I see. She wants you to know how much she's grown.

Jane: Wait, you mean grown since she died? She got taller?

Psychic: Yes, she is doing all this great emotional work.

Jane: They do that? Dead people, I mean? Ok, well, that sounds good. Anything else?

Psychic: Yes, hold on (more silent eyes-closed-head-nodding). I'm getting a clearer picture, I can really see her more clearly. She had silver curly hair, didn't she?

Jane: Maybe that's someone else's mother. My mom had long, straight brown hair.

Psychic: Uh huh. Uh huh. Yes, she wants you to know that she is making positive changes.

I'm not sure why hearing about Jane's experience didn't put a cap on the plan for me. I mean, really! The truth is though, I thought it might be a win/win situation. Either I would have a mind blowing experience that would nudge me towards the belief that there really is more than this earthly life ...OR, like Jane, I'd have a great story for a dinner party or for when I decide I want to be a stand-up comic.

Google search: Medium, contacting dead relatives, 5 stars, Portland, Oregon, on Zoom

First experience: I picked someone who had a 4.9 out of 5 point rating, worked on Zoom, and was $1/minute. I wanted to ease in and take it slow. Her name was Kat and it turns out she was in Albuquerque, New Mexico but she assured me that the spirits didn't care about distances and were fine on Zoom, something it hadn't occurred to me to ask.

Since I am such a bratty skeptic, in experiences like

this I never want to give away even the tiniest bit of information. It's at least one way to see if it's all legit, right? I mean, if you're really psychic, why do you need *me* to give you a name? So when she asked me who I wanted to contact, I said, "Someone in my family," and when she said, "Who?, "I said, "Anyone," and when she said, "Give me a name," I said (relenting because the clock was ticking and I just knew this wasn't going to go well unless I gave in a little and also because the name is sufficiently non-gendered so it still might not be giving her more information than I wanted), "Lee."

The medium did the close-eyes, rock-in-the-chair thing, taking her time (after all, I was being charged by the minute) and then said, "It's a woman. And she's very unhappy. She's telling me that no one understands her, that other people have all the luck, and that things never work out for her."

Holy, mother-loving shit! I ended the session right then and there. Too freaked out. Six minutes in, six dollars spent. And for six dollars, I'd heard from my mother. My mother, Lee. If someone asked me what my mother would want to tell me from beyond, it would be exactly that, exactly what she always said when she was walking around here on earth. "I'm very unhappy, no one understands me, other people have all the luck, and things never work out for me."

Mind blown.

Second experience: I decided to give it another try just to see if the first one was a fluke or a lucky guess or if it's the case that all mothers who die are unhappy and feel like no one understands them and everyone else has all the luck and that things never work out for them. This time I chose someone local who also had great reviews and who worked mostly as a medium rather than, like, a tarot card reader. I booked a 30-minute session with Amber and did my best to bring my most open-minded self to our meeting.

Again, I am asked who I would like to contact and again I'm ready to dissemble and throw up some kind of smoke screen but no need. Amber is ready to jump in. She says, "I'm hearing 'father, father, father.' Is that who you want to contact? I see someone in suspenders and a short-sleeved shirt, standing in a field."

There is *so* much wrong about this. My own father would have never–in his real, alive, walking around life at least–worn suspenders or even a short-sleeved shirt. Never! He was a New Yorker in the advertising business and may never even have *seen* a field. Also, no! That's not who I want to contact. It's a long story but I'm not sure I could have said a more adamant *no* which, given she's psychic, Amber picks up on it and actually probably should have known already. She lets it go and continues to ask who I want to contact. I finally give in since already the 30 minutes are ticking away. "My mother and my husband," I say and we are off and running.

This is where it gets mighty disconcerting. Amber asks if there is something about my husband related to the stomach. Yes, there is. She asks if it was cancer. Yes, sadly, yes. She says it was going on for a long time but he ignored it. Yes, damn him, yes. She says he is an emotionally stable, conscientious, slightly by-the-book kind of guy. Yes, yes and yes. She tells me he continues to be worried about the family and is looking out for all of us. The last thing she said, which is why I ended the session even a little early, was to ask if "he liked books, *too*." Okay, woman, that word gives you away. My email, which is where she sent the appointment information, has a link to my website at the bottom which is where, were you so motivated, you could gather some information on me including the fact that I am a writer.

What to do with this mishmash! First the absurdity about my father. Then the stunningly on-target stuff about my husband and how she could possibly know any of that is a total mystery. Followed finally by that apparent tell, which to me implied a not-so-psychic bit of info.

What to do with it all!?

But okay, just because I don't want to be a total brat with my mind clamped shut, I will give it one more chance.

Third experience: A friend suggested I try a tarot card reading so sure, why not. There's a cool store not far from where I live where I've bought some gorgeous crystals, not exactly because I believe they have special powers which, who knows, maybe they do, but because they are so, so pretty and it feels good to hold them. This store also books appointments with psychics, etc. so I made a 30 minute appointment with Kayla and here's how it went:

Kayla: Do you have any particular questions you are wanting to explore?

Me: (Takes me a beat because it's somehow a bit embarrassing to say it out loud). Yes, I do. I want to know what will happen to me after I die.

Kayla: Ok, that's a big one. Let's see.

Kayla shuffles the deck and asks me to cut the cards

at which point she lays three cards down on the table between us.

First card: Death (!!!!!!) (upright)
Second card: The Star (upright)
Third card: The Moon (reversed)

I am sufficiently freaked out even without having a clue about what these cards suggest and then Kayla went on to tell me what it all supposedly means. The death card signifies a transition of some kind. The star card represents hope and renewal. And the moon card (reversed) has something to do with overcoming a fear of the unknown.

I can go home now.

I suppose I could explore more. But why? Odds are probably between 99.99-100% that I would have the same mixed bag experience: some yowza stuff and some oh-come-on crap. That said, I do believe that the bits of astonishment in each of these experiences has scooched me at least a little bit closer to the idea that there just might be more to this whole shebang. I'm not so clear on exactly what's comforting about that, but it is. Maybe it's about significance. Maybe it's about what can otherwise feel like a desolate loneliness. Maybe it's about wonder. The awe of it all is, for me, so beautifully incomprehensible. And the swell of that feeling is so, so lovely against the contraction of fear.

True—I didn't leave these experiences in total awe-struckness. Fragments of awe, maybe is more accurate. What I do know, though, is that wonderment does not seem to coexist with fear. Contradictory states.

So, psychic guides: thank you for reminding me just where to set my guidepost.

16

WHAT'S THE ALTERNATIVE?

I could not possibly be more sure: I do not, not, not want to die. You tell me if I'm wrong but I guess the only other option is to live forever.

Which, of course, is insane.

What would that look like anyway? I keep getting older and older? Crinkled up and bent over till I'm the size of a two-year old? Periodic cataract surgeries and a full set of dentures, I guess. Knee replacement upon knee replacement. Three strands of hair left on my dried up scalp.

Or I stay this same age in perpetuity?

Either way, everyone I know would die and I would remain to mourn their loss. Over and endlessly over again. Loss upon loss upon loss. A more lonely, grievesome existence I cannot imagine. Not to mention the need to make a whole new crop of friends every, what, twenty or thirty years? I'm not great at that to begin with in this one blink of a lifetime.

No, I do not want to live forever. No.

It's binary: you live forever or you die.

I know, I know. Die I must.

17

MY DOG BILLY

I have Joaquin Phoenix to thank for nudging my life in a new, unexpected direction. Yup, that guy. Maybe not the ideal or expected role model choice, I know. Of course, I must have been ready, but it was his speech at The Oscars in 2020 that catalyzed a change in my life. Here's part of what he said:

"I think that we've become very disconnected from the natural world, and many of us, what we're guilty of is an egocentric worldview—the belief that we're the center of the universe. We go into the natural world and we plunder it for its resources. We feel entitled to artificially inseminate a cow, and when she gives birth, we steal her baby, even though her cries of anguish are unmistakable. And then we take her milk that's intended for her calf, and we put it in our coffee and our cereal."

That date—February 9, 2020—was the last time I ate any meat, the first time I made a righteous effort to limit any animal product at all.

Please believe: I know I risk coming off as self-righteous and polemical.

Also, you might be wondering what in the sam hill this has to do with death. I will get to that. Promise.

Just a few months after that Oscar speech, I saw a Norwegian movie called *Gunda*. This is an extraordinary film which I urge you to see if you can find it. The movie follows the life of a pig named Gunda, her piglets, and several other farm animal families over the course of their lives. There is no narration or human dialogue, no music. All animals, no people. All in black and white. I know that might sound uber-boring. Quite the opposite, in my opinion. Going by the effect it had on me, I can assume that the filmmakers set out to create a visceral and emotional connection between the viewer and the animals by simply (!) portraying their daily routines and experiences as they live their lives and interact with each other on the farm, including their struggles and moments of joy.

Maybe you pause on the word "joy" because maybe you think that is going too far down the anthropomorphic fantasy rabbit hole. I'll just say, agree to disagree. For me, this film is a non-militant plea to rethink our relationship with animals—beings that we might tend to dismiss as subservient and only valuable because we use them as food or handbags or, at the very best, as our furry companions. I'm deep enough into this mindset that—in spite of the good lives I believe I give my dog and cat—I often feel pangs of despair and guilt that my cat has never been able to hunt in the outdoors and my dog has to walk around on the end of a leash.

All this to say that the shift which had taken root earlier that same year was reinforced, my commitment growing even stronger.

And then there is this from Jane Goodall: "You cannot share your life with a dog and not know perfectly well that animals have personalities, minds, and feelings."

Maybe there are still two or three people out there who doubt that animals have feelings and personalities; that they can experience pleasure and pain and fear. Not me, and probably not you either. I stand squarely in the camp that believes that animals have feelings, personalities, and yes, thoughts. Maybe not thoughts in the way we human animals have thoughts, okay. But I have not a shred of a doubt that my dog Billy and my cat Mac are sentient beings—beyond sentient, too. Consciousness, sapience, maybe even an understanding of self. Who knows. And I believe this is true for non-mammals, too. If you've watched the movie *Fantastic Fungi* or *My Octopus Teacher* or read the book *The Overstory*, you might also agree with me that all living organisms are sentient. Even coral have an awesome intelligence!

Did you listen to the Fresh Air interview with climate journalist Zoë Schlanger about her book *The Light Eaters: How the Unseen World of Plant Intelligence Offers a New Understanding of Life on Earth?* The New York Times calls it "...a book that takes readers on a deep dive into the fascinating world of plant life, revealing a complex and awe-inspiring reality that forces us to re-evaluate our understanding of agency, consciousness, and intelligence; suggesting that plants, instead of mimicking human intelligence, might have developed their own parallel system of perception and response." Schlanger explores some mind-bending science about how plants learn, communicate, and adapt to survive. She even demonstrates how plants can store memories, trick animals into not eating them, and send alarm calls to other plants. It is utterly astonishing, and yet another rebuke to the speciesism that Joaquin Phoenix called us out on in that Oscar speech.

All of this brings me to panpsychism and how it relates to my obsession with death. You know that synchronistic thing that happens when you are focused on something and then you begin to see it pop up all over the place? There's actually a name for this: the Baader-Meinhof phenomenon, or "frequency illusion." (Note: I am NOT talking about the creepy way that A.I. and the web start showing you ads for sheets after you were making your bed, just thinking about the ratty set that needs replacing.)

The simplified explanation of the Baader-Meinhof phenomenon is that it is our awareness that has increased, as opposed to the new thing actually appearing more frequently. We develop a kind of lens that magnifies and highlights what we are focused on.

That's me and panpsychism. I guess since it was so much at the forefront of my mind, I had a more fine-tuned awareness and was much more likely to notice when it popped up on my Instagram feed, on my Google homepage, and then in an article in *The New York Times*. But whatever the explanation, I am seeing more and more written about panpsychism these days, and so I had naively assumed this whole phenomenon was a relatively new and trendy notion. Not so.

There are conflicting accounts of how and by whom the term "panpsychism" was first coined. Some accounts say it was the Italian philosopher Francesco Patrizi in the 16th century who attempted to replace Aristotelian physics and cosmology with a new understanding of nature. Other accounts say it was German philosopher Georg Wilhelm Friedrich Hegel in the early 19th century. But it is, in fact, one of the oldest philosophical theories and has been ascribed to philosophers including Plato, Spinoza, William James, Alfred North Whitehead, and Bertrand Russell. In fact, in the 19th century, panpsychism was the default philosophy of mind in Western thought.

The most pithy definition of panpsychism is the view that the mind, or a mind-like aspect, is a fundamental and ubiquitous feature of reality—a feature which exists throughout the universe. All things—animate and inanimate alike—have a mind-like quality. I know! It's not easy to swallow.

Here is a quote attributed to the Chinese philosopher Lao Tzu, who lived in the 4th century BCE and was the founder of Taoism:

"This world is indeed a living being endowed with a soul and intelligence... a single visible living entity containing all other living entities, which by their nature are all related. Who, then, is animate and who inanimate?... In the case of grass, trees and the soil, whether they merely lift their feet or energetically traverse the long path, they will all reach Nirvana."

Maybe you've had a glimmer of this Nirvana. My beloved animals, the thrum of the Wildwood trail, the images from the James Webb telescope—they all settle in my body with a sense of oneness and life, a glimmer of a belief that there is little difference between stardust and tree and rabbit and rock and flesh.

Here's Timothy Leary:

"The fact of the matter is that all apparent forms of matter and body are momentary clusters of energy. We are little more than flickers on a multidimensional television screen. This realization, directly experienced, can be delightful. You suddenly wake up from the delusion of separate form and hook up to the cosmic dance. Consciousness slides along the wave matrices, silently at the speed of light."

The cosmic dance. Can't you just feel the wonder of that!

And before I get more clear on how this has affected my terror of oblivion, there's another factor in the mix to explain. I think it was a mash-up of the pandemic, the heightened political mishigas after the 2016 election, and my own aging self. I've just become less and less pedantic and less and less wedded to my heretofore self-assured opinions. I've tended to attribute my bullheadedness to being a New Yorker and an Aries, if you put any stock in that, and yeah, there's also whatever unresolved childhood issues I live with.

But whatever the reason, I think I've had a tendency to be close-minded, defensive, and know-it-all-y. These last years have worn down some of those sharp edges, and now I find myself saying *who knows* to just about any possibility. It is, for me, a time of don't-know mind. I read this in Maria Popova's wonderful newsletter, *The Marginalia*, and I am inclined to agree: "Nothing, not one thing, hurts us more—or causes us to hurt others more—than our certainties." D'accord!

My new-ish Who Knows mindset is complicated, though. It is most definitely not purely a picnic at the beach. Yes, there was a (delusional) sense of safety that came with being wedded to my opinions. Yup, I know how I feel and what I believe. For sure, there is comfort in that. Who Knows is more of a mixed bag. My grip on certainty has loosened; rigid beliefs have softened; and for me, that is a much more vulnerable place. Who Knows is awesome—and I mean awesome in both meanings: awesome, as in inspiring feelings of reverence, and also awesome, as in inspiring fear. Anything could be possible. Anything! Eek!

The way all of this is related to my obsession/fear about death is this: While I never pretended to actually know things like: Is there life after death? Or is there life on other planets? Or are we in a simulation? Or is there a God?—you can bet your boots I had my strong opinions (read: pronouncements). Now, as I swim in the who-knows-ness of it all, anything seems possible. Maybe our consciousness lives on eternally; maybe we will reincarnate; lordy, maybe there actually is a heaven and a hell. Or maybe it's lights out—period, end of sentence. Ba-bye!

At this point in my life, what I am experiencing is that the more I am able to maintain a Who Knows stance to the big questions, and the more I sense the ubiquity of life and consciousness, the less freaked out I am by the thought of annihilation. Maybe death actually does mean annihilation. Maybe it does not. Maybe there is life after death. Maybe not. Maybe there is a God. Maybe not. Absolutely anything seems possible.

What I do know is that this collision of factors creates in me a nascent (emphasis on the word "nascent," please) sense of peace about my singular and brief existence in this particular bodily form. Because who knows.

Truth is, I can't quite hold on to this equanimous view. It is fleeting and, hard as I try to hold on—and do believe I try—my grip is elusive. Just when I think I have it in my clutches, poof, I am back to a more anxious mindset.

But, thanks to whomever or whatever, I do have Billy to help.

18

YOU SURE LOOK LIKE
MY MOTHER BUT…

I lived most of my adult life dreading the time when my mother would die. I dearly, dearly wish it were because of what you might be imagining—what you might have felt yourself about the eventual death of your own mother. I envy you. I really do.

I envy you if the thought of your own mother's death is too heartbreaking to imagine; that the loss of your mom would be so very devastating; that her death would leave you with unyielding grief.

Bless her heart, my mother presented herself to the world as the most important, special, talented person in the room. Her need for attention was mammoth. Here's a small example among a zillion: years ago, my mother was visiting me and I invited a friend over to join us for dinner, someone with whom I'd recently taken a trip. So far so good, until I made the fatal mistake of saying, "Hey, Mom, do you want to see the pictures of our trip?" And what else could my mother say but sure. So I fetched the photos (pre-iPhone days) and wasn't past picture three when my mother—without saying a word—stood up and went upstairs.

Okay, maybe she needs a sweater or forgot to take her pills or I don't know what. But after 20, 30 minutes she's not back downstairs. Weird. And after 45 minutes, it was clear she wasn't coming back downstairs to join us. You might think I am overdetermining this, that I am stretching the point beyond credulity. But I could bore you to tears with the boatload of examples I have of just this thing: when the attention was not on her for an extended time (in this case, ten minutes), she just could not seem to bear it.

So that's one factor that had me wondering—and frankly concerned—about how my mother might handle a fatal illness. Also, there's this: I do not think there was a single visit, a single phone call, a single interaction I had with her where she did not complain about some undiagnosed ailment, an unsympathetic doctor, a collection of inattentive nurses, waiters, bank tellers, store clerks, you name it.

All of this left me with visions of a nightmarish hospital scene, with her yelling at nurses, throwing food on the floor, pressing the call button again and again and again. The whole hospital staff praying that she would just fucking die already.

So much for my fears and predictions. In the short time between her diagnosis and her death, my mother was the most calm and equanimous I'd ever known her to be. You could not imagine a lovelier, sweeter, more agreeable person. In those last hospital days, there was laughter, teasing, ballerina pink nail polish, and even (gasp) flirting with the doctors. I cannot even conceive of anyone seeming less afraid of what the next days would mean—and she was well aware of what they would mean.

A giant relief for me, oh yes. A relief and a surprise and yet another indication that my experience of this mother of mine was not all there was to her. Maybe in those last days she was able to release her ego and put down the heavy cloak of narcissism. Maybe she finally breathed some freedom. Maybe her life had just been too hard to bear. How sad is that.

Here's a letter I wrote *after* she died:

> *Dear Mom:*
>
> *I am so sorry.*
> *You told me you weren't feeling well. Of course, you always said that, that you weren't feeling well. We heard that all the time.*
> *But still.*
> *You said you had some kind of bump thing on your stomach but this time it's a bump, last time it was a sharp pain, before that a strange sensation in your head, three years ago you had a toothache the dentist wouldn't or couldn't help you with, and before that your psychiatrist didn't care that you were depressed and on and on. In fact, I don't remember a time when you didn't have a bump or a pain or a weird feeling or a disinterested doctor or a dizzy spell.*
> *But still.*
> *You told me it was a pretty big bump, a soft lumpish thing as big as your fist. I said what I always said, you'd*

better go see your doctor. He said what we all said, what we all believed. It's nothing. It's a benign sebaceous cyst, just some fluid-filled thing that will go away on its own but go ahead and use a warm compress, couldn't hurt.

Two weeks later you were dead.

Afterwards they determined it was lung cancer but only after following the scavenger hunt of clues that eventually led them back to the original source.

They started at the bump—not a sebaceous cyst but a malignant tumor, big as your fist, big enough that you could see it through your clothes from across the room. The next clue was hidden in your liver so I guess that explains the pain in your side, huh. From the liver to the bones, the muscle cramps in your left leg you complained about over and over and over again and finally to the lung cancer that had metastasized into every organ in your body.

I am so sorry.

But still.

I mean, what did you expect? There was the time your other daughter left work, found someone to watch her infant daughter, drove the choked Bay Bridge into San Francisco in rush hour traffic only to find that no, actually you were fine, you didn't mean to scare her when you said you'd just called 911, you hadn't actually done that, she'd misunderstood. Or the time you called her at 3 a.m., you sobbing so hard she had no way of knowing what you were saying, trying to figure out what was wrong and finally getting in her car and again crossing the Bay Bridge into the black San Francisco night to find you fast asleep. Or the time on the first day of one of my visits that you told me you had been gushing blood every time you went to the bathroom—your word, gushing—and I called your doctor who told me to take you right to the ER where, after sitting in the straight-backed chairs for two hours, when it was finally our turn, you told the doctor that no, not really, you actually hadn't been bleeding, you didn't really know why you were there but you came because I wanted you to. This is how it went.

But still.

This time. This one time. And what we did was roll our eyes and slam down the phone and swear and commiserate and hate you all over again.

But how you were at the end. In so many ways not the mother we had known. And it wasn't just the absence of bluster and bombast. So much grace, an ease we'd never seen before. The mother I'd dreamt of, here at the end.

I am so, so sorry.

Even still.

Love, Liz

All of this to say: Mom, it's clear I did not know you. The way you approached your death, well, unforeseen is the understatement of understatements. I can only wish that I have the kind of grace you had when it's my time. Maybe this is a neon-light example of how none of us can be entirely known.

Also, this is a regret I will live with. Maybe you could have helped me. Maybe if I'd asked. Maybe if I'd opened my heart to you, my heart that had been covered over by a carapace of hurt and anger and disappointment–maybe you'd have helped me; taught me what it takes to be so equanimous at this most weighty crossroad.

What a loss for me and for you, too. What a loss for us both. A chance in those final moments to heal just a tiny bit. Oh, well. Another in a long line of missed opportunities for us. I am grateful, though. I am grateful for the gift you gave my sister and me at the end–how we could be with you without the white hot anger we were so used to. How we could see you at peace, finally at peace.

My whole walking around life with you was so fraught. The end, though: a blessing.

19

READING LIST

My reading taste tilts toward fiction but as I was working on this project I read all the non-fiction books about death I could get my hands on. Most were at least a little bit off-target for the exploration I was most interested in: attitudes people have about their mortality and how they might find more peace as they approach the end. Many of the books are about grief and how to deal with the loss of a loved one. Some focus on the medical aspects of dying and what happens to our bodies when we die. Some focus on spiritual/religious factors which were a bit more on target. There are, of course, many more books on the topic than I have listed. It's clear to me that I'm not the only one interested/fascinated/daunted by the reality of our deaths.

Here is the current list, most of which I highly recommend; none of which did much to allay my fear. Oh well.

- *Being Mortal* by Atul Gawande
- *Stiff* by Mary Roach
- *Mortality* by Christopher Hitchens
- *When Breath Becomes Air* by Paul Kalanithi

- *How We Die* by Sherwin Nuland
- *The Whispering Door* by TJ Klune
- *The Midnight Library* by Matt Haig
- *Staring at the Sun* by Irwin Yalom
- *Tuesdays With Morrie* by Mitch Albom
- *The Violet Hour* by Katie Roiphe
- *Advice for Future Corpses* by Sallie Tisdale
- *Nothing to Be Afraid of* by Julian Barnes
- *The Denial of Death* by Ernest Becker
- *Nothing to Fear* by Julie McFadden, RN
- *Life After Life* by Raymond Moody.
- *Will My Cat Eat My Eyeballs* by Caitlin Doughty
- *Things I've Learned From Dying* by David R. Dow

20

NDE. YES, PLEASE.

In 1892, a Swiss mountain climber named Albert Heim collected the first accounts of near-death experiences (NDEs) from 30 fellow climbers who had suffered near-fatal falls. Most, he said, experienced a sudden review of their entire past, heard beautiful music, and "...fell in a superbly blue heaven containing roseate cloudlets."

That sounds nice, huh.

Ernest Hemingway had a brush with death in World War I when he was serving as an ambulance driver on the Italian front, during which he sustained multiple shrapnel injuries from mortar shell explosions. He later wrote about the experience, saying, "...dying is a very simple thing. I've looked at death, and really I know. If I should have died it would have been very easy for me. Quite the easiest thing I ever did."

Later, in his famous story *The Snows of Kilimanjaro*, the protagonist knows he is dying after contracting gangrene on a safari gone very wrong. After flying through a storm with rain as thick as a waterfall, the plane emerges into the light and he sees before him "...

unbelievably white in the sun, ...the square top of Kilimanjaro. And then he knew that it was there where he was going."

Hemingway's description shares all the elements of a classic near-death experience: the darkness, the cessation of pain, the emerging into the light, and then a feeling of peacefulness.

That also sounds nice.

In researching the NDE phenomenon, I was fascinated to learn about a man I'd never heard of and wish I had known about earlier: John C. Lilly. Lilly was a neuroscientist, psychoanalyst, inventor, and a bunch of other titles I could name. He was also a compatriot of counterculture figures like Timothy Leary, Ram Dass, and Werner Erhard. Lilly is credited with developing the isolation tank, doing groundbreaking research with dolphins, and engaging in some other pretty far-out stuff. And that's just a small smattering of things I could tell you about this fascinating man.

During one experiment in a hot tub, Lilly nearly drowned and later recounted his experience, which confirmed for him "...that his life was guarded by higher powers in the extraterrestrial reality, a hierarchy of entities operating through the control of coincidence on a global scale." He later came to call this his NDE experience.

There was scant interest in exploring the NDE phenomenon until Raymond Moody burst onto the scene with his 1975 book, *Life After Life*. Lest you feel inclined to scoff at this topic and are tempted to think he might be some sort of quack, Moody completed his Bachelor's Degree with honors in Philosophy from the University of Virginia; a Ph.D. in Philosophy; and an M.D. from the Medical College of Georgia. No slacker, this Dr. Moody.

Moody's interest in near-death experiences began while he was an undergraduate at the University of Virginia in 1965. It was there that he met the psychiatrist George Ritchie and heard his story. It seems that when Ritchie was a young army recruit, he contracted pneumonia and was ultimately pronounced dead. Nine minutes later, the attendant who came to take him to the morgue thought he detected chest movement. After a shot of adrenaline into his heart muscle, his pulse returned and Ritchie started to breathe, regaining consciousness after four days. He later wrote a book—*Return From Tomorrow*—where he describes what later would be called a near-death experience.

It seems that hearing Ritchie's story was all it took for Moody, who then began documenting similar accounts by people who had experienced clinical death and, lo and behold, he found that many of these experiences shared common features: the feeling of being out of one's body;

the sensation of traveling through a tunnel; meeting dead relatives; and seeing a bright, beautiful light.

In his, albeit controversial, book, Moody explores personal accounts of subjective phenomena encountered in the near-death experiences of people who had apparently died and then been resuscitated. He became what you might call a true believer, saying in an interview: "I don't mind saying that after talking with over a thousand people who have had these experiences, and having experienced many times some of the really baffling and unusual features of these experiences, it has given me great confidence that there is a life after death. As a matter of fact, I must confess to you in all honesty, I have absolutely no doubt, on the basis of what my patients have told me, that they did get a glimpse of the beyond."

Another prominent pioneer in this field of study is the psychologist Kenneth Ring. In 1980, Ring published his book, *Life at Death: A Scientific Investigation of the Near-Death Experience*, which is considered a foundational text in the field. In it, he outlines what he determines to be the five stages of a near-death experience:

- Peace and well-being: A feeling of peace, contentment, and absence of pain.
- Separation from the physical body: A sense of detachment from the body, which can progress to an out-of-body experience.

- Entering a transitional region of darkness: Entering a tunnel-like experience.
- Seeing a brilliant light: Seeing a light that some describe as mystical or otherworldly.
- Entering another realm of existence: Entering a heavenly environment through the light.

Not too long after Moody's book popped onto the scene, a group of researchers created *The Journal of Near-Death Studies*, a scholarly peer-reviewed, cross-disciplinary journal that builds on his work and—boom—the field was off and running. Here's just a small smattering of articles published in this journal:

"A Prospective Analysis of Near-Death Experiences in Cardiac Arrest Patients"

"The Ketamine Model of the Near-Death Experience: A Central Role for the N-Methyl-D-Aspartate Receptor"

"A Neurobiological Model for Near-Death Experiences"

"Near-Death and Out-of-Body Experiences in the Blind: A Study of Apparent Eyeless Vision"

"Near-Death Experiences: A Neurophysiologic Explanatory Model"

"Flight of Mind: A Psychological Study of the Out-of-Body Experience"

"Psychophysiologic Correlates of Unconsciousness and Near-Death Experiences"

It didn't take long after Moody's book emerged for NDE studies to split into diverse schools of belief. There were —and are—the spiritualists, some of them evangelical Christians, who are convinced that NDEs are genuine sojourns into the land of the dead and the divine. Spiritualists believe in a continued future existence after death and that people who have passed into the spirit realm can communicate with us flesh-and-blood folks here on planet Earth. Their aim, it seems, is to collect as many reports of near-death experiences as possible and to proselytize about the reality of life after death.

Moody is their most important spokesman and—yes, this might sound a little out there to some (I know not you, Shirley MacLaine)—he eventually claimed to have had multiple past lives. In fact, Moody went on to build a "psychomanteum" in rural Alabama where people could attempt to summon the spirits of the dead by gazing into a dimly lit mirror. These, um, facilities still exist and you can even build one of your own if the spirit moves you (see what I did there?).

The second, and largest, faction of near-death researchers were—and are—the parapsychologists who, by and large, are trained scientists who follow well-established research methods. Their interest is in phenomena that seem to undermine the scientific orthodoxy that the mind cannot exist independently of the brain. They tend to believe that NDEs offer evidence that consciousness can persist after death. Many of them are physicians and psychiatrists who have been deeply affected after hearing the near-death stories of their patients.

For me, the most compelling example here is none other than Carl Jung. In 1944, Jung suffered a near-fatal heart attack. In his book *Memories, Dreams and Reflections*, he describes the event in detail, in part saying this: "It seemed to me that I was high up in space. Far below I saw the globe of the earth, bathed in a gloriously blue light." He goes on to describe encountering a temple where he would "...at last understand this too was a certainty what historical nexus I or my life fitted into. I would know what had been before me, why I had come into being, and where my life was flowing." After this life-altering experience, it seems that Jung would often recall the "sting of disappointment" at being brought back to life, saying, "Life and the whole world struck me as a prison. I had been so glad to shed it all."

To many in the parapsychology world, death is not an ending, not oblivion, not annihilation. It's more like moving from one realm to another.

Finally, there are the physicalists. This is a small contingent of scientists who are committed to a strictly biological account of NDEs. Like dreams, the physicalists argue, near-death experiences might reveal psychological truths, but they do so through hallucinatory fictions created by the workings of the body and the brain. Their basic premise is this: no functioning brain = no consciousness = no life after death. Their task is to discover what is happening during near-death experiences on a fundamentally physical level.

Perhaps the most prominent of the physicalists is Dr.

Jimo Borjigin of the University of Michigan. Her studies have found that the brain is highly active during cardiac arrest, and that brain activity in the moments before death is different from what has been previously thought.

Here's Dr. Borjigin:

"A lot of people thought that the brain after clinical death was inactive or hypoactive, with less activity than the waking state, and we show that is definitely not the case. If anything, it is much more active during the dying process than even the waking state."

Borjigin's work provides scientific support for the theory that NDEs are caused by a surge of electrical activity in the brain, and that an elevated level of brain activity could give rise to near-death visions.

In one study, patients who were taken off life support showed a sudden increase in gamma waves—the type of brain wave that usually indicates conscious thought—in a portion of the brain that is right on top of the visual cortex. Commenting on the research, Dr. Jason Braithwaite of the University of Birmingham said the phenomenon appeared to be the brain's "last hurrah."

There's another bigwig in this field that deserves mention. Bruce Greyson is a psychiatrist who has built on Moody's research and is often dubbed the father of research in near-death experiences. Greyson has done extensive, peer-reviewed research, which found that the most commonly reported effects by those who experience these kinds of events are loss of fear of death; strengthened belief in life after death; feeling especially favored by God; a new sense of purpose; increased self-esteem;

increased compassion; and less focus on material gain and status, among several other wonderful things.

What I wouldn't give to believe all of that!

Greyson also developed what is fittingly called the Greyson Scale of NDEs. This is a self-report questionnaire which sets out to measure the depth of an individual's near-death experience. Greyson's intention was to develop a tool which could be used to differentiate NDEs from stress responses and organic brain syndromes. From my vantage point, I am not clear on how this questionnaire accomplishes that particular goal or, in fact, how different using this instrument might be from a simple interview. At base, it seems to be an effort to bring some scientific cred to the field which, gotta say, seems like a very steep hill to climb.

Take a look and see what you think:

THE GREYSON SCALE

1. Did time seem to speed up or slow down?
   - 0 = No
   - 1 = Time seemed to go faster or slower than usual
   - 2 = Everything seemed to be happening at once; or time stopped or lost all meaning
2. Were your thoughts speeded up?
   - 0 = No
   - 1 = Faster than usual
   - 2 = Incredibly fast

3. Did scenes from your past come back to you?
   - 0 = No
   - 1 = I remembered many past events
   - 2 = My past flashed before me, out of my control
4. Did you suddenly seem to understand everything?
   - 0 = No
   - 1 = Everything about myself or others
   - 2 = Everything about the universe
5. Did you have a feeling of peace or pleasantness?
   - 0 = No
   - 1 = Relief or calmness
   - 2 = Incredible peace or pleasantness
6. Did you have a feeling of joy?
   - 0 = No
   - 1 = Happiness
   - 2 = Incredible joy
7. Did you feel a sense of harmony or unity with the universe?
   - 0 = No
   - 1 = I felt no longer in conflict with nature
   - 2 = I felt united or one with the world
8. Did you see, or feel surrounded by, a brilliant light?
   - 0 = No
   - 1 = An unusually bright light
   - 2 = A light clearly of mystical or otherworldly origin
9. Were your senses more vivid than usual?
   - 0 = No
   - 1 = More vivid than usual
   - 2 = Incredibly more vivid

10. Did you seem to be aware of things going on elsewhere, as if by extrasensory perception (ESP)?
    - 0 = No
    - 1 = Yes, but the facts have not been checked out
    - 2 = Yes, and the facts have been checked out
11. Did scenes from the future come to you?
    - 0 = No
    - 1 = Scenes from my personal future
    - 2 = Scenes from the world's future
12. Did you feel separated from your body?
    - 0 = No
    - 1 = I lost awareness of my body
    - 2 = I clearly left my body and existed outside it
13. Did you seem to enter some other, unearthly world?
    - 0 = No
    - 1 = Some unfamiliar and strange place
    - 2 = A clearly mystical or unearthly realm
14. Did you seem to encounter a mystical being or presence, or hear an unidentifiable voice?
    - 0 = No
    - 1 = I heard a voice I could not identify
    - 2 = I encountered a definite being, or a voice clearly of mystical or unearthly origin
15. Did you see deceased or religious spirits?
    - 0 = No
    - 1 = I sensed their presence
    - 2 = I actually saw them
16. Did you come to a border or point of no return?
    - 0 = No

- 1 = I came to a definite conscious decision to "return" to life
- 2 = I came to a barrier that I was not permitted to cross; or was "sent back" against my will.

All of this so far presents NDEs as these almost blissful experiences. Who wouldn't want to feel peace and well-being and then be bathed in a mystical, brilliant light? But, to be fair and honest and above-board, it seems to be true that not all NDEs are positive. It may be that these less-than-wonderful experiences are underreported due to fear, shame, and social stigma. The prevalence of these not-so-great NDEs is somewhere between 1–22%, but some of the reported features are pretty unsettling—things like encountering lifeless, threatening, or evil beings, or finding oneself in harsh or hellish environments. Again, these less-than-wonderful experiences do seem to be in the vast minority and, to be fair and honest and above-board, I don't really care about those cases.

What I cling to here is the possibility that my little pea-sized existence is not a meaningless blip. And, most importantly by far and away, is the conclusion of Moody's research and others that followed him: the most salient aftereffect of an NDE is a decrease, or even loss, of fear of death. In fact, in studies that followed his where participants were explicitly asked about their fear of death post-NDE, between 80% and 100% reported a marked decrease. And an Australian study in 1990 found that 100% of participants reported no fear of death post-NDE. No fear! 100%! None!

Believe me, I am not jonesing for a near-death experience. Do you hear me, universe? This is not me manifesting. That would qualify as going way, way too far to ease my fear. BUT. It turns out that much of what is experienced after an NDE can apparently be achieved by taking a hero's dose of ketamine.

Note to self.

21

TALKING TO ANGELS

As of this writing, I have spoken with four hospice nurses and three death doulas. What an unmitigated blessing that these anointed ones are roaming the earth among us.

Lucky you if you haven't had the need to reach out to a death doula or a hospice nurse. It seems more likely than not that the vast majority of us eventually could use the help of these skilled professionals. In a fair world, all of us would have access.

There is overlap for sure, but death doulas and hospice workers or nurses have different training and different roles.

A death doula, also known as an end-of-life doula or death midwife, provides emotional, physical, and informational support to individuals who are nearing the end of life and their families. Among probably a whole host of other things, they can:

- Offer emotional support in the form of comfort and companionship.
- Facilitate conversations about death, providing a safe place for people to talk openly.
- Help with logistics like completing advance directives, funeral planning, and coordinating with healthcare providers.
- Talk to people about the process of dying, options for care, and what to expect.
- Help create meaningful and personalized end-of-life ceremonies.
- Offer respite time to family caregivers.

In short, death doulas support the whole family by attending to their spiritual, emotional, and physical needs. What a blessing.

A hospice nurse has specialized medical training in providing care for people who are in the final stages of a terminal illness. There is overlap in approach and function with death doulas, but hospice nurses are primarily trained to:

- Care for patients by administering medications and managing symptoms like pain and nausea.
- Make continual assessments of the dying person's condition and adjust care depending on need.
- Offer emotional support and education to help navigate the end-of-life process.
- Educate everyone about the dying process, prognosis, and available resources.

- Coordinate care with doctors, social workers, and spiritual advisors.
- Be an advocate for the dying person's wishes, making sure their preferences are honored.

Death doulas and hospice nurses: The world owes you so much gratitude that you have chosen this path.

Sidebar: Can we pause for just a sec, though, to think about why it would be that 100% of the hospice workers and death doulas I ended up speaking to are women; and 100% of the hospice workers and death doulas I reached out to for interviews are women; and a Google search of hospice workers and death doulas in Portland, Oregon, yep, 100% women. Something to wonder about, at least. And also midwives. Of course, it'd be beyond creepy to have male midwives (mid-husbands?). But think about it. Women bring us in and they take us out.

I am deeply grateful that the death doulas and hospice workers I reached out to were willing to take the time to speak with me. To a one, they were gracious and open, lovely and generous with their time. I had done my research and had enough personal experience to understand the job descriptions and the similarities and differences in their respective roles. What I was most curious about in reaching out to them was to hear their stories about the emotional state of people who are close to death. I had this kind of double-edged motivation.

On the one hand, I expected all my personal attitudes and feelings to be confirmed. I was prepared for them to tell me that the people they worked with were distraught and anxious; that they could hardly contain their panic and that most deaths they witnessed were far from peaceful. I thought these women would recount scenes of skeletal hands grasping their sleeves, guttural cries of "I-don't-want-to-die-save-me-no-no-no." I thought they'd tell me story after story about how they consoled fear and anxiety.

You've guessed right if you think I've been projecting myself onto that hospital-bed-in-the-living-room tableau.

On the other hand, I was hoping against all my instincts that they would tell me quite a different story; that most of their clients and patients left this world in peace and acceptance; that, if you put any stock in the Buddhist philosophy, their calm and stress-free death assured them a peaceful transition and a more fortunate rebirth—something much, much, MUCH more fortunate than what I fear I might end up as, i.e., being reborn as a pigbutt worm.

Back to the point, though. What I heard from the hospice workers and death doulas I spoke with was not what I was expecting or fearing. What they told me was much more like what I was hoping against hope to hear. Granted, this is a small n sample, so just how generalizable are their experiences? Well, what the internet tells me is: very!

All of these seraphs had a similar tale to tell. And as they told me their stories, it made sense in a way that, for some weird reason, hadn't quite occurred to me before but now seems so frickin' obvious.

Insert sound of me smacking myself in the face.

By the time you qualify for hospice care, you have a terminal illness, typically with a life expectancy of six months or less. It is most likely the case that every time you turn around, you're being poked and prodded and stuck and jabbed. The indignities abound. You've probably spent endless time in doctor's offices and hospitals. You may have had multiple surgeries, interventions, medications, etc. A bedpan might be a reality. Your life has most likely shrunk down to a micro-sliver of what it was. You are likely exhausted and might not even recognize the sunken-faced stranger you see in the mirror—that is, if you have the strength or the will to even look. And if all of that is true, there may hardly be any room left for fear. In fact, you may actually be craving a time of no needles, no hospitals, no exhaustion, no nausea, no tests, and no pain. You might actually look forward to the relief of death. You might just be flat-out done.

Please don't get me wrong, and whomever in the universe may be listening, I am most definitely not hoping I'll be in hospice care anytime soon. Fingers crossed that I die in my sleep at a ripe old age from a painless event preceded by zero hospital stays or surgeries or debilitating illnesses. That said, what I heard from these folks who are so up close to the end with people was comforting in an unexpected way.

I mean, I always knew that hospice was a blessing. My own husband was made so comfortable and pain-free in his last days. I was able to bring him home to die because

—and only because—hospice would be coming to help. In his drugged and/or near-death mind, we were in a forest in Russia—random, I know—but as a seasoned traveler and citizen of the world, he was decidedly jazzed about this. He even seemed happily surprised when our cat jumped on his bed. "This is amazing," he said. "Even Dodger is here with us!" This was the first cogent (?) sentence he'd spoken in weeks and the last words he'd ever utter, the cancer having metastasized to his brain and, oh my my my, how beholden I am to—to what? To whom? I have zero idea about what created that delusion or vision: cancer cells? Morphine? Endorphins? Spirits? God? Or maybe it wasn't a delusion. I don't give two hoots! Twenty-five years later, that clear-as-a-bell sentence, that look of wonder on his face—while the holes in my aging brain are draining away so many of my memories—that one will endure.

Also, I can't say I know this for sure, but his death may even have been gently urged along by the judicious and generous and more-than-prescribed use of morphine. (Promise I won't tell, dear hospice worker.)

I'm kind of embarrassed that what these hospice workers told me, and what now seems so obvious, had just not occurred to me.

The oblivion thing? That's still what it's about for me. But whatever mental picture I've held of myself—me lying in a hospital bed, wracked with pain and in a state of utter panic—well, consider that picture to have modified a click.

I can visualize the scene—hoping, of course, that conjuring a picture doesn't work some manifesting juju.

But when it is my time, let it be this: I've got the hospital bed in my living room, a room with floor-to-ceiling windows in the southeast corner of the building. So much light, so much sky. My dear animals are here and my cherished children, my beloved grandson, their presence and their touch, deeply felt. It wouldn't be my children, though, without laughs that make my stomach hurt and please let that be the last sound I hear.

All this while the angel assigned to me adds more morphine and then a little more.

22

LESSON LEARNED

On the night before the day my mother died, I didn't sleep. After she'd dozed off, or slipped into unconsciousness, or partially died, or whatever it was—that state she was in—I walked back from the hospital to spend the night at her place.

I could practically stand in one spot and touch the four walls of this, her last sad home. She had left this place the way everyone had, and the way everyone would leave here. Once you get to a place like this, you can forget about the future.

She'd only lived there a few months, but already her place was overrun by paper. She had two file cabinets full of papers; cardboard boxes of papers; grocery bags stuffed with paper; stacks of paper on every flat surface. There was so much paper, you barely noticed the safety rails and help-me-I've-fallen buttons and the kitchen with the mini-fridge and Easy-Bake Oven.

Maybe that was the point—try to block out the evidence, pretend you're just living in a normal home. Or maybe holding onto paper felt like holding on to evidence of a life.

But if you ask me, it was another in her very impressive repertoire of indirect ways to communicate. Here's what I mean: I opened a file folder marked "Important Papers." In that folder, I found the deed to her house three houses ago, a contract from her health insurance company (no longer valid), and a copy of the title for her dead husband's car that was sold, let's see, about fifteen years earlier. Really, Mom? The file marked "Receipts" could barely hold its contents. Receipts from Macy's and Safeway and Nordstrom. From Pacific Gas & Electric and Golden Dragon Dim Sum and AT&T and 7-Eleven. Bus tickets and movie tickets and dry cleaner receipts. And then, in an unmarked grocery bag on the floor of her closet—about halfway down into the truly, utterly junk—I found a copy of her will. Her goddam current, valid will! There she is, half a mile away, dying, and can't I just have my sorrow? Must you infuriate me, woman!

And then there was this: in a file folder labeled "Misc" I found what turned out to be an active life insurance policy, which, of course, we knew nothing about. Here is a taste of the Mr. Toad's Wild Ride I had to go on to figure out that little issue:

> Me: Hello. I'm calling about a life insurance policy of my mother's, policy number XFG-27765-MG.
>
> Insurance Person #1: Date of birth?
>
> Me: 11/19/25.
>
> Insurance Person: That's not the date of birth I have listed.
>
> Me: But that's on her driver's license. What do you have?
>
> Insurance Person: I can only give that information to the policyholder.

Me: But she's dead. My mother. That's why I'm calling.

Insurance Person: Any other documents?

Me: Hold on………okay, yeah, I've got her death certificate. It says 11/19/27.

Insurance Person: Nope. That's not it.

Me: Wait, wait. 11/19/24, that's on her state ID.

Insurance Person: No.

Me: Can I guess?

Insurance Person: I don't care. If you want.

Me: Well, how much is it for, the policy? What's it worth?

Insurance Person: I can only release that information to the policyholder.

Me: She's..Oh, nevermind. I'll call back

Me: Hello. I'm calling about a life insurance policy, my mother's policy number XFG-27765-MG. She's…

Insurance Person #2: Date of birth?

Me: Ok, that's the thing. I have three different dates and I guess they're all wrong and the other lady wouldn't tell me.

Insurance Person: Ok, no problem. We can do it another way.

Me: Oh good, thank you.

Insurance Person: Just send us a copy of the birth certificate.

Me: I don't have a birth certificate.

Insurance Person: You'll just have to order one then.

Me: Look lady, I don't know the name of the town and I don't even think the country still exists, it was just this dinky little foreign place from the stone ages– like a shtetl– and I don't even know what her real name was. There is no birth certificate. Never mind. I'll call back.

Me: Hello. I'm calling about my mother's life insurance policy and before you ask, I don't have the right birth date and...

Insurance Person #3: You can just fax the birth certificate.

Me: Look, I don't have anything like that and I can't get it. There. Is. No. Birth. Certificate. I'm begging you, please. Can I just guess the date?

Insurance Person: I guess.

Me: 11/19/18?

Insurance Person: That's not what I have.

Me: 11/19/20?

Insurance Person: Nope.

Me: 11/19/21?

Insurance Person: No

Me: Am I getting warm?...never mind, 11/19/22?

Insurance Person: Yes, that's the date of birth we have in our records.

And, yes, I ended up getting half her life insurance money but taking into account the number of hours I put into sorting through all that shit I figure it equaled a reimbursement rate of about $1.25/hour.

But all that paper, all that nonsense? I know what she's saying. She's saying: *You can't get rid of me that fast, Missy. You're going to have to stay with me detail by detail. Bit by bit. Scrap by scrap.*

It's not like there was anything new in her attempts to demand attention. Au contraire. Still, a funny thing to say by a woman who withheld from my sister and me even the tiniest details of her history. Including her date of birth.

But okay, lesson learned.

By now, my kids are tired of being reminded about the fireproof box under my bed—*I know, I know, mom!* Every time I take a trip and then again if it's been awhile, I remind them about the box, where it is, where the key is, and what's in it:

  i. The names, addresses, and telephone numbers for my attorney, my financial advisor, my insurance agent, my CPA, and my closest friends
  ii. My will
  iii. A detailed Advance Health Directive
  iv. A copy of my driver's license
  v. Account numbers and contact information for all financial holdings
  vi. Credit card numbers
  vii. A list of all pin codes and passwords
  viii. Information on my mortgage

    ix. Pre-paid arrangements for what to do with my body
    x. My passport
    xi. Appraisal for a string of pearls
    xii. Long Term Care Insurance policy
    xiii. The title to my car
    xiv. Valuable coins and silver certificate bills
    xv. Two small gold ingots
    xvi. My wedding ring
    xvii. Eight 100-dollar bills

You've heard this advice: get your affairs in order. This appeals to me on a bunch of levels. First, I don't like clutter. Second, I do not want to burden my kids the way—well, you know. And C, if I get my affairs in order then I'd be an A+ student, right? And maybe I get extra points and then maybe...?

But magical thinking aside, what I do believe is that I have off-loaded some guilt about causing my children more agita. I do believe that this is a way of shedding and of readying myself. And I do believe that whatever I can unload before the end will ease my way along.

23

CLOSEST I'VE COME FOR REAL
(EXCEPT FOR THE CHOKING THING)

My phone rings at 8:30pm on a Thursday night. No name on the caller ID but I recognize the prefix. 413. Legacy Health. Calling me at 8:30pm on a Thursday night.

On Wednesday–the day before–I'd had a breast biopsy after a routine mammogram was inconclusive, as was the follow-up ultrasound. Inconclusive but clearly suspicious.

Someone at Legacy Health was calling me at 8:30pm on a Thursday night.

I could just let it go to voicemail.

Because if I don't answer and just let it go to voicemail and then not listen to the voicemail, I could–you know how that works–prevent anything bad from happening. *La di dah, la di dah*.

On the last ring before voicemail I pick up.

"This is Dr. Blah-bitty-blah. Your biopsy results are in."

Of course I know. Maybe my brain that has suddenly become mush doesn't know, but my body does. Because he did *not* say, *"Just* calling to give you the results of your biopsy," where that word *just* does so much work which is why I don't speak because I can't really speak or think because he didn't say *just*.

"Are you there?" he says. And I think maybe I should hang up.

"Sorry, yes, I'm here."

"The biopsy was positive."

And now I've missed my chance to hang up and have it all go away.

I say, "You mean positive, like cancer?," like there might conceivably be some other meaning, like maybe positively wonderful.

"Yes. I'm sorry. Yes, you have cancer."

This followed by that kind of telescoping feeling. That sense of everything, every little thing, collapsing into that one pinpoint, the place where there is not a single other thing but the one thing that is: *You have cancer and you are going to die.*

Followed by: *I'm not ready, I'm not ready, I'm not ready.*

I had my surgery, my six weeks of radiation and my five years of estrogen-blocking drugs.

During which: *I am scared, I am weak, I am a coward.*

That was ten years ago. I am fine, knock on wood. The thing is, though, what's left is this sense–to my regret and shame– of how I will be when the inevitable comes. I do know I've made progress on the road to equanimity. I want to reinforce whatever strides I've made. Give myself the pats on the back that I've earned. That said, this experience definitely felt much more Susan Sontag than Ram Dass.

24

JUST SAY YES!

I was 74 when I became a psychonaut.

The ratty sweatpants with the drawstring waist were the most comfortable thing I could find. And a deacdes-old waffle-knit, long-sleeved top that was loose enough in the arms that I could push up the sleeves if I got too hot, long enough that they could keep me warm if need be—because who knew what the need would be; certainly not me. No bra. I followed the hard-for-me instructions: no food, no caffeine, no juice; only water beforehand. I dropped my dog at a friend's house and set out.

Angel—not her real name, but I'll call her Angel because I truly think that's what she is, and also because what she does is illegal—lives in the hills of Portland, in a neighborhood kind of new to me, set against a stage of trees, all in their springtime verdant glory. It was a gorgeous day—the kind of blue-sky prize of a day that we people in Portland suffer for after months of unrelenting rain and gray skies. And there she was, waiting for me at the door, looking every bit the way you'd want your medicine guide to look: long, strawberry-blond hair in tight curls, gauzy white clothes, bare feet, and a smile that instantly quelled the nervous diarrhea that had been threatening me all morning.

"Beautiful one," she said, giving me the kind of full-body hug that is deeply satisfying and sadly rare in my current life. "I'm so happy you're here." She led me into a space that I'll try to describe, but I know I'll come up short and not be able to do it justice. You'd just have to see it.

Here was a very large room with cushions and soft mats and plush blankets and feather pillows—everything in various shades of Benjamin Moore white. Every corner, every space: lush and soft and gentle. It's as though the room had no sharp angles. Altars with candles burning and such beautiful music—somehow not the annoying spiritual kind that typically makes me want to ram chopsticks in my ears. I felt beckoned, as though the space were giving me the same deep hug. My body knew. This space is safe. This person is safe. I am safe. Each step into the room loosened up my gut, deepened my breath, deflated any temptation to flee. We are most definitely not in Kansas anymore.

Much to my deep regret and occasional shame, the '60s passed me by. I didn't wear tie-dye or long, flowy skirts or a puka shell necklace. I didn't go to the Poor People's March on Washington or see Resurrection City—even though it was during my junior year in college at George Washington University, which was close enough that I could have crawled there without scraping my knees. I didn't smoke weed until my mid-twenties. I didn't go to Woodstock, even though I was just 22 and it would have been a short drive. Not a counterculture chick, not a hippie or a yippie or a burner. I most certainly did not turn on, tune in, or drop out. I missed the whole fucking Summer of Love.

What I was doing instead was taking my micro-mini-skirted self to one frat party after another, skating by in classes just enough that I didn't get kicked out, and doing what I was there for: find the husband. Not one serious, self-aware bone in my skinny-assed body.

Just to put a fine point on it, I was working in a bookstore a couple of blocks from the White House on April 4, 1968, when, just as we were about to close, a brick came through the window and Washington, D.C., was soon in flames. Most of my friends had left town for spring break and were already slathering their bikini-ied bodies with baby oil in Nassau. It only took an hour or so before all the phone lines were down, and I had no chance to leave and, do believe, I wanted to leave.

The city was a hellscape. Anyone who was not as ditzy as I was back then might have taken to the streets and joined the outrage. For days the city was paralyzed with protest and violence—National Guard armed with machine guns and tanks on many corners. Buildings on my campus burned to the ground. Me? I spent the week in a pout. Nothing to do, nowhere to go, no friends to hang with. No parties. Definitely not your prototypical child of the '60s.

Oh, you dear, callow child, how much you have to learn!

Taking psychedelics had always been a scary thought to me. Not uninteresting, but most definitely scary. I don't think you'd ever have known that, though. In fact, you and I were both likely taken in by my bravado (read: defensiveness). Taking drugs was a sissy way of becoming a godhead. It was a shortcut, a lazy road to enlightenment. It just didn't count. I would go about it all in the real way, thank you very much! I'd explore my inner recesses with a clear head. As a non-addict, I'd borrow the fearless moral inventory from AA. I'd re-up with my take-no-prisoners therapist. I'd be brutally honest with my friends and family.

But really, I was scared. All the diagnosed and undiagnosed mental illness in my family was probably lying in wait, ready to pounce, hiding just over there behind the impressive coping skills I'd developed and the picture of mental health that I presented to the world.

I was legit scared that I would be the one who'd have a bad trip, but not only a bad trip. I could handle a bad trip. But I'd read the cautionary tales: people with incipient mental illness could be thrown into a place of disordered mind and permanent psychosis, never to return to normal.

Contrary to my lifetime experience of examining myself and my decades of work as a psychologist, there it was, whispering to me: *Girl, you might be a schizophrenic and just don't know it.* Maybe I'd fooled not only the world but myself, too. Maybe all my pathology would be revealed. And for what anyway? To see spirals and kaleidoscopes and talking animals? Yeah, that sounds kind of cool, but in no way worth the risk.

But my interest in entering into the psychedelic subculture kicked into high gear after my friend and I went to see *Dying to Know*, a documentary about the epic friendship between Ram Dass (Richard Alpert) and Timothy Leary. These two ex-Harvard psychology professors—both fired for their participation in the study of psychedelics—spent their lives championing the benefits of mind-altered states. For both these men, their experiences with psychedelics had been transformative, shaping each of their lives for decades after.

This wow of a documentary blasts through whatever preconceptions we might have about drugs and life, and the biggest mystery of all: death. From all accounts, both men met the notion of death without fear, even and especially as they got closer and closer to their own. They both (weirdly, I must admit) saw death as a celebration. In fact, Leary said, "I'm looking forward to the most fascinating experience in life, which is dying." And in Ram Dass's words, death is a time when you "...engage with the deepest meaning of the universe." And in several videos I've also heard Ram Dass say that dying is like "...taking off a tight shoe." Um, o.....kay?

But come on, were these guys really unfazed by their impending demise? Really? I'm a skeptic at heart and a New Yorker to boot, so I went on a search. I watched every YouTube clip of Leary and Ram Dass that I could find. I read every account of their final days and last moments: first-hand, second-hand, all of it. I was expecting to see some evidence of panic as their earthly lives were ending, some kind of *only kidding, folks*, some glimmer of deathbed panic. But nope. Ram Dass died in his home on Maui, peaceful and surrounded by loved ones. This from Rameshwar Das, his co-author and dear friend:

"If there was ever someone without fear of dying, it was Ram Dass."

And in an interview a few months earlier, when asked when he knew he was ready to die, Ram Dass said, "When I arrived at my soul. Soul doesn't have fear of dying. Ego has a very pronounced fear of dying. The ego, this incarnation, is life and dying. The soul is infinite." And Leary? When he learned he had inoperable cancer, he reportedly said he was "thrilled."

I gotta say, that sounds downright wacky to me.

Psychedelic plants and fungi have been used in indigenous medicinal traditions for millennia. In our country, there was burgeoning scientific curiosity and promising research into the effects of psychedelics during the '50s and '60s, especially focused on the use of LSD to treat addiction, anxiety, depression, and fear of death. In fact, Bill Wilson, co-founder of AA, credited his experience with LSD for helping his own recovery and depression.

All of this came to a screeching halt, and in large part we can credit Nixon's "War on Drugs." In 1970, he introduced the Controlled Substances Act, rendering psilocybin, mescaline, LSD, and DMT illegal. Bye-bye, Ram Dass and Timothy Leary.

Of course, much as I'd like to lay all the blame on Nixon, the excesses of the drug culture were understandably scary, all those long-haired crazy kids. There's that, too.

But after a long puritanical winter, psychedelic spring has come. The times they are a-changin', my friends. In this post-prohibition era, research into the therapeutic uses of psychedelics has taken off with a vengeance. There is a gathering momentum again, and a new wave of U.S. clinical trials into all sorts of drugs with psychedelic properties.

In 2022, over 1,000 brain scientists gathered in San Diego for the annual meeting of the Society for Neuroscience. The topic? Psychedelics and neuroplasticity. They were there to learn how these drugs could help rewire the brain and offer new treatment for conditions like chronic pain and depression. The Johns Hopkins Center for Psychedelic and Consciousness Research is backed by $17 million of funding, and their work is exploring a wide range of uses for these compounds—depression, PTSD, and anxiety, among others.

Sounds pretty mainstream to me.

All this to say: there was a confluence of factors at work for me. That said, I may not have been as ready to take the psychedelic plunge even after seeing that very persuasive movie and reading about all the promising research, had I not also become an officially old person. Death was right out there at the tip of my fingers, and I was not, not, NOT happy about it.

To be clear, it wasn't the dying part. I may be deluded, but I do believe there is enough morphine and plenty of sympathetic hospice workers out there. So even though I know many people are afraid of the dying part—the pain and the indignities—not me. For me it is the *being dead* part. The annihilation. And right there, to my shame and horror, might just be—who knows—my legacy as the daughter of two parents whose pictures you can find in the DSM chapter on narcissism. How can *my* life cease to exist? How can who *I* am dissolve into nothingness? How am *I* simply like every other life form on earth? And please tell me this: How can the world keep spinning without *me* in it?

Boy oh boy, if Ram Dass is right that ego = fear of dying, well, my ego must be ginormous.

I could not deny that the challenge of getting more comfortable with my mortality was an important project for me to wrap my arms around. At the very least, I sure have had plenty of motivation to avoid the extremely unappealing Sontag model of dying.

Yes, I was on the path to psychedelic readiness, and the nudge that pushed me right over the edge appeared in a journal article detailing a study done at Johns Hopkins where about 90% of the participants in a psilocybin trial reported a significant decrease in their fear of death.

Ready!

The first time I met with Angel, we talked about the various plant medicines available for me, how they are different and the same, and what I might expect from each. If you knew me, you would not be surprised to hear that I went home and plunged into some deep-dive research about the choices she was offering me.

Ayahuasca: People close to me have had ayahuasca experiences and, while they—to a person—reported these to be very profound and meaningful, there was also psychic pain and fear. Not to mention the vomit! Me = too much of a baby.

MDMA (AKA molly, E, ecstasy): I'd had two previous experiences, which were groovy for sure, but it just seems like more of a party experience—think raves with EDM. Not what I was after.

DMT and 5-MeO-DMT: Both of these are naturally occurring, endogenous psychoactive compounds, which exist in numerous species of plants and animals, including we human animals. DMT is often referred to as the *spirit molecule*, while 5-MeO-DMT gets the moniker of *god molecule*. I've read them described as two best friends with slightly different party tricks. Happily, my research led me to listen to everything I could get my hands on about and by Terence McKenna, an American ethnobotanist and mystic and all-round fascinating man.

I was most interested when he talked about his experiences with DMT this way:

"Why this is not four-inch headlines in every newspaper on the planet I cannot understand, because I don't know what news you were waiting for, but this is the news that I was waiting for."

While these drugs are related, there are major differences in effects. DMT tends to produce more intense visual experiences (look up the weirdly common phenomenon of encountering *machine elves*) while 5-MeO-DMT tends to produce concentrated shifts in perception.

Psilocybin: your magic mushrooms. From all I read, the effects could be just about anything, including feeling giggly, euphoric, energized, paranoid, anxious, panicked, overwhelmed, or just about any other feeling you could name.

Rightly or maybe naively, I believed that psilocybin would be the best place for a skittish novice to start.

Journey #1: Angel sat cross-legged across from me and held both my hands. It was surprisingly easy to hold her gaze, even in silence. Those greenish-gray eyes. Hard to explain how some eyes can hold so much kindness. We breathed. For several minutes, all we did was breathe. And soon, my quick, shallow breath matched her grounded breathing.

In her preparatory instructions, she'd asked me to

meditate on my intention for the experience. Easiest thing so far: *Let go.*

Sidebar: As a psychologist and as a human, I firmly believe that the skill and practice of letting go is a lifelong, ubiquitous, universal, recurrent challenge for us all. From the jump, there are a zillion ways we are called on to let go of what we might be grasping on to: relationships, jobs, health, appearance, certainty, life, etc., etc., because, like the Buddha says, everything changes, and change almost always comes with the need to let go.

Angel said, "Do you feel ready?"

"I am, yes," I said, not entirely sure I was, in fact, ready. When she left the room to brew my heroic dose of psilocybin tea, I gave myself one more talking-to. *You can leave, you know. You're a grown-ass woman, and no one can stop you if you don't want to do this.* But it was such a puny voice, an echo or maybe even artifice. It was a voice with no sway.

I know I am not alone in finding it hard to put words to psychedelic experiences. In some ways, I believe it to be a nonverbal experience. I was there for a few hours, though the concept of time was meaningless. Most of the time, I was lying on a plush mattress on the floor with the covers over my head. I did not see visions. I did not have hallucinations. I had what I can only describe as an observational platform from which I was viewing myself. *Oh, there's that defense, there's that block. Remember this, it will help you if you remember this.* Such a gentle ally, a *me* and a *not-me*, with the sole agenda of answering questions I hadn't even formed yet and offering advice I didn't know I needed.

When I finally felt able to move, and then lift off the covers, and then even sit up, Angel was waiting with water and a plate of fresh fruit, which might have been the most amazing thing I had ever tasted. She helped my shaky body out to her porch and, oh my, had there ever been a more beautiful blue sky, or a more delicious warm breeze, or a more dizzying flourish of green: the leaves on the overhanging tree, so many shades of green.

I don't know how long we sat there in our perfectly comfortable silence, but what would have been my usual social awareness—neurosis—was absent, along with any need to move before I felt entirely ready. That, in and of itself! A miracle.

I was so grateful that neither of us felt any pressure to talk, analyze, describe, or interpret. That time on her porch, on a spring day of perfection, might be the most stress-free, demand-free, expectation-free time of my life.

My existential terror? Maybe a tick less, but I left with a fellow traveler—a *me* and a *not-me*, an ally a step or two ahead on the road.

I waited about nine months until I felt ready again, and then it was time to contact Angel.

Journey #2: I felt skittish about the machine elves thing because, in several accounts I'd read, they could be taunting and degrading and downright terrifying. Case in point: the YouTube video of Joe Rogan talking about how the machine elves taunted him, screaming at him, calling him a "fucking idiot"—maybe deserved, but still.

But machine elves aside, it was the shift in perception

that often occurs in a journey using 5-MeO-DMT that seemed like what I was after. A shift from death = paralyzingly terrifying → death = okay, whatever.

Again, Angel and I sat together, close and facing each other. We breathed; she smiled; I glued myself to the cushion so I wouldn't flee. She explained what would happen: crystals would be vaporized in a pipe, and I would inhale through this glass straw. I would immediately feel the impulse to lie down, so she placed a pillow in the exact right place for my head. The whole experience would be less than 10 minutes, and I would feel completely awake and aware when it was over. It seemed so odd and freaky and inconceivable and scary that the powerful experiences I'd read about could happen in less than 10 minutes. Turns out, yes!

Angel was right. I felt wide awake, clear-headed, and fully cogent after what felt like an eternity but was actually eight minutes. My first words to her: "You're not going to ask me to explain this, are you?" Because, truly, it was inexplicable. I will say this: I know I gasped with awe. I know I was astonished. I know it was profound. I also know that any time I have been tempted to explain my experience, it all sounds so trite and mawkish.

Truth is, I have always believed that there are things that defy language—that words can cheapen or diminish some particularly profound and extreme events. I want to hold dear this experience. I want to guard against anything that may debase and trivialize it.

The best I can do is to tell you this: there was the most beautiful silver light. There was a knowingness of being woven into the fabric of the universe, a deeply felt experience of oneness. These are feelings that still live in me. If I quiet myself and place myself in that room, with that dear, dear soul, I can access those feelings today—not as intensely, of course. But they abide. They live here in my body. And yes, what they say about the shift in perception—I felt that.

I don't yet know how to measure the impact these journeys had on my fear of death, what scale to use. More rock-chipping, I guess. (Which, by the way, is how I talk about the therapeutic process with my clients: chipping rock.) But I have felt, at minimum, a subtle shift, especially after the mind-blowing interaction with 5-MeO-DMT. You might snicker—I know my inner cynic tends that way. But this was my true experience: there is beauty everywhere, the universe is in us all, and love is everything.

Yes, yes, and for sure, yes. My discomfort about my own mortality is still there but, hard as these things are to measure, I'd say I've continued to tick down in the journey from terror to garden-variety fear. The way I felt so integrated into the fabric of it all. The astonishing beauty. Rock-chipping, maybe, but it's so often how this kind of emotional or psychological work seems to move—in almost undetectable bits.

This I believe: even if the movement might not seem obvious from the outside, that doesn't mean that shifts—important shifts—aren't happening.

I will keep chipping away, and when death is closer, you can bet I will be knocking at Angel's door.

25

THAT'S ME IN THE CORNER, CHOOSING MY RELIGION

God, I am beginning to realize, might just happen to be a pivotal character in this death obsession psycho-drama of mine. There does not seem to be a way to extract religion from any deep dive into mortality and whatever, if anything, is next after my time on terra firma.

I wasn't raised with any religion. Well, we went to the Northfield Congregational Church on Christmas and Easter and during a week in August when my mother was in charge of the Antiques Fair. But going to a Congregational Church is like going to a meeting of the National Pie Club. That's how far from doctrinaire it is. At least that's my fairly ignorant, three-times-a-year impression.

In my family, there was no religious conversation and, even more to the point, no real discussion about values and morality and those other things that are often the cornerstone of any religion, let alone of a life well-lived. It wasn't until I was in my 30s with two small children that I learned we were actually Jewish, and not just Jewish but Jewish with a capital J. Thirty-three generations of Rabbis on my mother's side. And counting. Both of my parents were Jews and both were either disowned by their families or maybe they were the ones doing the disowning. Add that to the list of things we never talked about and will never know. But once this pretty compelling and, wouldn't anyone think, vital information came to light, well, I've got questions!

There was not a relative in sight when my sister and I were growing up. No grandparents, aunts, uncles, cousins...nothing! I remember when I was a kid asking my mother if she had any brothers or sisters. Her response? *I don't remember.* Somehow, amazingly, gobsmackingly I accepted that as an answer. So, we grew up with no extended family, no knowledge of all those generations of rabbis and no faith tradition or grounding in the constellation of beliefs and practices that I assume go with most religions.

I often wonder how my feelings (read: dread) about my mortality would be different were I a believer. In anything. That's a bit too harsh, of course, and also not accurate. I believe in family and friends. I believe in animals. I believe in kindness and fairness. I believe in love. It's just that stacking these beliefs of mine up against what gets inserted into the spongy brains of little kids in Sunday school just does not seem to have the same currency and by that I mean it doesn't buy me anything in the everlasting eternity department.

Drum roll please: Enter Blaise Pascal and his famous wager. This 17th century French mathematician, philosopher, physicist, and theologian posited that individuals essentially engage in a life-defining gamble regarding the belief in the existence of God. Pascal's argument is based on several strands of thought, including:

- Probability theory and decision theory
- Pragmatism

- Voluntarism i.e. the idea that belief is a matter of the will, and
- The concept of infinity

Pascal's wager goes like this:

- If God exists and you believe: You gain infinite happiness in heaven.
- If God exists and you don't believe: You lose infinitely, either by going to hell or being separated from God forever.
- If God doesn't exist and you believe: You lose nothing.
- If God doesn't exist and you don't believe: You gain nothing.

Simple conclusion: It won't cost you anything to believe in God so go ahead, why not.

Pascal, my man. You make sense. But, you yourself called it a gamble so I wonder exactly which religion might just increase the odds of easing this unsettled mind of mine.

I have a dear friend who was raised Catholic. Deeply Catholic. Nuns all the way and a Catholic college to boot. When she lost her beloved mother, yes, she grieved. Yes, she was so sad that they wouldn't have their Christmas cookie-making extravaganzas or their annual trip to Vegas to play the nickel slots. Their daily phone calls. But she knew, she *knew*, she would be seeing her mother again. She was deeply comforted knowing she would be reunited with her mother in Heaven.

This is what I–the skeptical-at-best psychologist–unofficially diagnose as *Chronic, Undifferentiated Catholicism*. You may be thinking this is a slam on the religion. It's not. More, it's about how deeply embedded these teachings are when one is exposed from an early age and for many years after. But any perceived snark aside and please forgive, how nice that must be. If I could only force-feed that certainty. Poof! Death as a passageway to reunite with your dearest ones in a fluffy white cloud eternity. Fear? What fear.

I know it is too late for me to be a Catholic. I don't have decades of education that would ground me. I haven't grown up with a community of like-minded folks who share these deeply held beliefs. I haven't devoted hours upon zillions of hours studying the texts. The soil of my baby mind was not prepared and tended to in a way that these beliefs could grow and thrive. In my more ungenerous moments I might call that brain-washing or indoctrination. But that also may be because there is envy in my heart. How amazing would it be to actually believe!

Gotta say, though, it's the dogma that would trip me up, even if I could. Correct me if I am wrong but if you believe you will see your mother again in Heaven, isn't that because you have a foundational belief in resurrection? I can totally groove with the metaphorical way of thinking about re-birth and Heaven and afterlife but I doubt that would make me a real Catholic and I absolutely know that the metaphors don't do me a dang bit of good in this quest for a more equanimous attitude toward my mortality.

So, it's no to Catholicism but it may just be that understanding how other religions think about death and the afterlife (if any) could help me come to more peace. But please, please understand: these are cursory, overly-generalized, kindergarten-level summaries. I could write a whole, uneducated book about the so many sects and divisions in each of these religions. I ask you to please forgive if I have short-changed/misrepresented/or warped your particular system of belief. Absolutely zero offense intended. Yes, true...I have been accused of snark that can teeter too closely to disrespect. Asking forgiveness for this as well. Oh, and yes, these might be the biggest but they are only the tiniest fraction of the religions out there. In fact, *Wikipedia* tells me there are roughly 10,000 religions in the world. Who knew!

Here's the most cursory–and it probably couldn't be more cursory– look at the main contenders:

CHRISTIANITY

- Belief in the Afterlife: This seems to be the cornerstone, the whole belief in the afterlife thing, and the one that I might groove with the most if I could just get there. For sure, the thought of a guaranteed afterlife would be consoling. So I'm listening, Christians. Tell me more.

- Jesus. That's not me swearing, that's what it's all about. Jesus and dying on the cross and resurrecting. The resurrection of Jesus Christ is the central, symbolizing victory over death and the offering of hope for an afterlife. This seems to be such a core tenet and, truth be told, a real stumbling block for me. But for Christians, the death of the physical body is not the end and, just like for Jesus, there is the promise of eternal life after death.

Well, I'd have to get clear on exactly what that means. If it were about Jesus as a lovely human with solid progressive principles, then sure, all aboard for that. But it does seem that it's more about Jesus as a kind of super-magical being and if that's a required belief in order to have everlasting life, well, I guess I am shit out of luck. Not to mention the whole the virgin birth thing.

- Heaven, Hell and Purgatory: Heaven and Hell and Purgatory seem to be real actual places for many Christians. Not like Hawaii is heavenly... or that your root canal was Hell. Actual places like if they were on Earth they'd have a zip code. Heaven is a place of eternal peace and joy so why fear death if that's what's in store for you? Of course, you'd have to lead a good life and if you do, it's off to Heaven to live with God in eternity. On the other hand and a more dicey prospect, if you are a sinner, Hell awaits where you are separated from God and live out eternity in torment. And what distinguishes a good life from a not-so-good life, I'm not so clear. St. Peter, it seems, is the one who separates the wheat from the chaff and sends some (and I'm afraid I'd be among the 'some') down below. And then there is Purgatory, a state of temporary punishment where you hang out, I guess, until you've learned your lesson and repented.

The Verdict: Too much to swallow and too judgy.

ISLAM

- Pre-Judgment Day: After death, most Muslims believe that the soul will enter *Barzakh*, a state of waiting that precedes the Day of Judgement. When a person dies, their soul is taken by *Azra'il*, the Angel of Death. God sends two angels, *Munkar* and *Nakir*, to question the waiting soul. The questions posed to the individual encompass fundamental aspects of Islamic belief, including:

1. Belief in Allah: The deceased is questioned about their faith in the one true God and is basically on trial to suss out the sincerity and depth of their belief.
2. Belief in the Prophet Muhammad: The questioning also includes the extent to which the dead person accepts the prophethood of Muhammad as the final messenger of Allah.
3. Deeds and Actions: Individuals are asked about their actions and deeds during their lifetime. This encompasses a wide range of ethical and moral conduct, including acts of kindness, charity, honesty, and adherence to Islamic principles. (Reminds me of Albert Brooks' movie, *Defending Your Life*–a movie I love–but without the focus on Islam.)

The dead person is then made to stand upright in their grave and asked to identify Muhammad. Already this is a little, um, scary but there's more. The righteous will be able to identify Muhammad as God's messenger and are rewarded by being allowed to rest peacefully until Judgment Day. Sinners, infidels, and probably me, will be unable to answer correctly and will be beaten by the angels every day except Friday. YEESH! This is really intense, y'all.

- Judgment Day: And now on to the actual judgment. It is Allah aka God who ultimately evaluates people on the Day of Judgement, not those two angels. Each person's actions are assessed by Allah so I assume this means that the two angels of pre-judgment Islam have a similar job description as the Christian figure of St. Peter who's the one pointing up or down in judgment.
- Allah weighs the deeds of each individual and then decides whether that person's *'ākhirah* (afterlife) lies in *Jahannam* (Hell) or *Jannah* (Heaven) on the basis of the weight of either good or bad deeds in comparison with one another.

The Verdict: Too scary!

HINDUISM

- Reincarnation: Hindus believe in the cycle of birth, death, and rebirth (*samsara*). The *atman*, or soul, is eternal and undergoes rebirth until it achieves *moksha* (liberation) and poof, you are then free from the cycle of rebirth. Actions in this life affect future lives which hopefully encourages moral living. Humans may be reborn as animals if they repeatedly fail to learn lessons in human form, which actually doesn't sound so bad to me, depending on the animal.

We're talking here about your *karma* which you've no doubt heard about in your yoga class or from being alive in the 21st century. But, once again, the atman may enter *swarg* (heaven) or *narak* (hell) before rebirth. *Karma* has some appeal, for sure. I throw around that term, often as a way of calming myself down about someone who seems to get away with all sorts of shit, especially one particular person I can think of. Sadly, when it comes to my own karma, well, I'm betting the best I could hope for is something from reptiles on down.

- Brahman: Hindus believe that *moksha* is the *atman* becoming absorbed with *Brahman*—the male, female, and animal source of all atmans. This concept of *Brahman* covers a lot of bases. Again, I turn to Wikipedia which describes *Brahman* as:
- "Eternal, unchanging, and omnipresent.
- The cause of all changes, yet unchanging itself
- The binding unity behind the diversity of existence
- The spiritual core of the universe
- Present in every atom of creation
- The only reality in existence
- The formless spirit from which everything comes
- The separate seeming gods of Hinduism, which are manifestations of Brahman"

The Verdict: Too risky, so it's a no to Hinduism.

BUDDHISM

- Impermanence (*Anicca*): Buddhism teaches us that all life is impermanent and that clinging to life causes suffering. (sidebar: BUSTED!)
- Rebirth: Similar to Hinduism, Buddhism believes in *samara*, the cycle of life, death and rebirth. The ultimate goal is to attain *Nirvana*, a state which frees one from this cycle.
- The Moment of Death: Buddhists believe that the attitude of the mind at the moment of death is very important and that it is vital to approach death with calmness and open-minded acceptance. The state of your mind as you are dying significantly influences your next rebirth, with a peaceful mind leading to a more positive future life according to the concept of *karma*; essentially, your final thoughts and emotions can shape your next incarnation. Just the pressure of this would guarantee that I would in no way, shape or form have a calm thought in my head. And my life as a slug would follow.

The Verdict: True, that's a Buddha statuette in my front hall but, nope. It's the whole karma risk again and I am positive I would fail the last moment of life test. At this point in time, I can no more imagine myself feeling peaceful and unafraid at the end as I can imagine myself summiting K2 without oxygen.

Shintoism

- Survival of the spirit: Shintoism does not believe in reincarnation. Instead, the spirit of a deceased person becomes a *kami*– a god-like

being that lives alongside humans by way of prayers and sacrifices made by their family. It's not clear to me what happens if your family doesn't want to make any sacrifices though.
- The Physical World: Shintoism in Japan emphasizes harmony, purity, fertility, and reverence for nature. Shintoists believe that the physical world is sacred and worthy of respect. They also believe that the universe is watched over by the harmonious cooperation of the *kami*. These *kami* are spiritual beings that are objects of worship and reverence and, after death, are believed to continue to exist and help the living. Apparently, after 33 years the spirit of a person becomes part of the family *kami* which are the spirits of ancestors believed to protect the living from harm. I'd have to know more, like is this family *kami* made up of my actual family, because the decades I already had with my mother (not to mention my father) were plenty, thank you very much.
- Otherworlds: The spirit of the dead dwells in otherworlds, and it's notable that these otherworlds are not described as a heaven or hell.

The Verdict: Big yes to the nature thing. And the thought of being an object of worship and reverence does have appeal, for sure. But there are some relationships I just cannot risk carrying into perpetuity.

TAOISM

- Life as a cycle: Taoists see death not as an end but as a transition within the continuous cycle of life, similar to the changing seasons in nature. When someone dies, their spirit is believed to live on and can move to another realm.
- Importance of living well: The quality of one's life on earth is crucial as it influences the nature of their afterlife. Unlike some religions, Taoism doesn't typically depict a single heaven or hell, but rather various realms depending on one's actions in life. This is not exactly like the concept of *karma*, though. For one thing, Taoists don't lean on a system of moral retribution based on actions like the traditional understanding of *karma* in Hinduism and Buddhism; instead, Taoists focus on living in harmony with the "Tao" (the way, the natural order) without getting caught up in notions of good and evil. That sounds nice.
- Ancestral worship: Many Taoists practice rituals to honor deceased ancestors, believing they can still interact with the living.
- Nature and Cycles: Death is often viewed as a natural part of the life cycle, interconnected with the environment and the cosmos. Taoism believes in an afterlife in this way: upon death, a person's spirit continues to exist and can migrate to another realm, often interpreted as a different form of life within the natural cycle. The ultimate goal is to achieve oneness with the Tao by living in harmony with the universe through ethical conduct and aligning with the natural flow of life.

The Verdict: Given how nice this sounds, I think it's kind of odd that I've never knowingly met a Taoist. Maybe they keep it under wraps which, for me, is another check in the plus column. A contender, for sure.

I've saved the most likely candidate for last. It's my birthright, after all. Had my parents not been disowned by their families (maybe that's what happened) or had my parents' families not disowned them (or maybe that's what happened, my sister and I never got the full story), most likely we would have grown up going to *cheder*, and then moving on to study Hebrew, getting ready for our *bat mitzvahs* by learning the blessings for the *aliyah* and chanting the *haftarah*. We would have griped about the pathetic bedazzled *dreidels* we got for Hanukkah while our gentile friends got Xboxes and a zillion other presents. We would know what blessing goes with what holiday and we'd be braiding *challah* every *Shabbat*.

This is so late in coming but I have hosted a Passover *Seder* for the past several years. I put together my own *Haggadah*, heavy on more spiritual sentiments with the Buddha even making an appearance. And there is poetry too. True, I need my cousin to sing the blessing and I only have the most bare-boned acquaintance with the details of the Passover story. That said, I look forward to this gathering. I find it meaningful and moving which sure makes me wonder if Judaism is embedded down deep in a way that's inescapable. Just might be my own version of *chronic, undifferentiated*.

It's a little head spinny for me, learning about the various sects and factions that fall under the rubric of Judaism. I could spend the rest of my life going down into this warren and then that one. And the information out there seems to contradict itself–sometimes identifying three, sometimes four, sometimes a bunch of different sects. As far as I can tell, the main branches of Judaism, at least in North America, are: Orthodox, Reform, Conservative, and Reconstructionist. But since this is not a three volume book on Judaism, or a dissertation, or even a journal article, here is a summary of what I've learned about how Jews relate to death and whatever comes next.

Judaism

- Afterlife Beliefs: Life after death is not a central belief in Judaism. In fact, Judaism is famously ambiguous on the topic. Yes, the immortality of the soul, the world to come, and the resurrection of the dead do figure prominently but the details are notably vague. How Jews live their lives on earth is considered to be more important than a possible afterlife. That said, Judaism has varied beliefs about the afterlife, including concepts of the World to Come (*Olam Ha-Ba*) and the resurrection of the dead.
- Heaven is not a gated community. The righteous of any faith are welcome. Our actions, not our specific beliefs, determine our fate. No concept of Hell exists in Judaism as far as I can tell. The closest we get is the fate of an apostate (a person who renounces God, faith and morality in this world), who is said to be "cut off from his kin." (Mom? Dad? Is this hitting a nerve?) This book would be double the size if I went on to discuss the various theories

about what exactly might be the consequence of apostasy. I will say, though, that the alleged custom of Jews to look at things from all angles and debate a zillion possibilities is another way I jibe with Judaism.
- Sheol: It was in post-biblical times that most ideas about the afterlife were developed. *Sheol* is a place of gloom and darkness that comes after death. The term can be interpreted to mean either the literal place in which dead people are placed (i.e., in the ground) or, in my opinion, more easy to accept, as a metaphor of the *Olam haBa* (afterlife). This is rarely discussed in Jewish life–Reform, Conservative or Orthodox. In the *Torah*–the most important Jewish text–there is no clear reference to the afterlife.
- Focus on Life: Judaism emphasizes living a righteous life according to God's commandments, rather than focusing heavily on death. The emphasis is on the exercise of human free will to do good work. "Repair the world" is the English translation of the Hebrew phrase *tikkun olam*, which means to actively work towards improving and fixing the world around you and a commitment to contribute to a better society. The idea is that living an honest, humble, and service-oriented life reduces the fear of death.
- Eternal Soul: The soul is considered eternal, and death is seen as a transition to be reunited with the Creator. Short on details here.

The Verdict: There just might be some ancestral resonance going on here. The Jewish way of thinking about death and what comes after is the least likely to freak me out, make me snicker or leave me dumbfounded. *Chronic, undifferentiated*? Yup, just might be. But, truly. Do I really think I can start going to temple, fast on the high holidays (that might be a deal breaker for real), or—Hashem forbid—no electricity on the sabbath?

I throw up my hands. Living an ethical life? Sure. Rituals, reverence for nature, good deeds? Yes, yes and mostly! Trying to be brutally honest here and sincerest apologies to the people I believe I must be offending. I just know I will never, ever, no matter what, be able to get to a place where I believe in Heaven or Hell or afterlife or even karma. If I could, I would, and do believe I've tried, but I just can't.

Religion, it seems, just won't be my ticket to a less bumpy ride to the end.

But wait!

Where God is concerned, I've labeled myself agnostic because who knows about *anything*, right? It's the old tried and true and perhaps wimpy strategy of hedging-one's-bets, God-wise. Of course this is the very obvious ploy of playing both sides against the middle.

Don't get me wrong, I have no trouble getting squarely behind the idea that there is some greater force at work in the universe. Of that I am not agnostic. But in the same way that I don't believe that gravity cares about what happens to me, I have to confess that it is too far for me to travel to believe that the greater force(s) of the universe gives a nano second's thought about me, or whatever approximation to *thought* might fit.

On the other hand, I have to admit that I feel a bit

timid about loud and proud declaring myself an atheist. It's so...um...so absolute, so unconditional, so box-me-into-a-corner, and not just any corner but a corner that might just have disastrous consequences. (I heard you, M. Pascal!) It's hard for me even to declare it in the privacy of my own head. But. Most religions seem to do their damnedest to deny death or, if not deny, then leave it an open question–the whole heaven, or karma or past lives or spirits kinds of things. How in the world to get behind that! And if I just cannot deny death as a reality—if I, in fact, see death as a finality—isn't that a denial of God?

If I were an avowed atheist, I would believe that after death there is *nothing*. Nothing, as in what there was *before birth*. I've never given a second's thought or anything within a lightyear of worry about what happened to me *before* I was born. That's even a weird thought...."what happened to me before I was born.." as if there were a "me" that something happened to. Here's Vladimir Nabokov on the subject in *Speak, Memory*: "The cradle rocks above an abyss, and common sense tells us that our existence is but a brief crack of light between two eternities of darkness. Although the two are identical twins, man, as a rule, views the prenatal abyss with more calm than the one he is heading for (at some forty-five hundred heartbeats an hour)."

So what's the difference? After I die, I will return to the nothingness that was my prenatal condition. I just may be on to something here. The rub, I am starting to think, is confusing *something* with *nothing*. When I am in an existential panic about my annihilation, I am thinking of *something*. Annihilation and oblivion are *something*. Floating around in a black, indifferent universe is *something*. Heaven and hell and spirits are *something*.

This deserves some deep cogitating. At first blush, I

am intrigued. But lordy, there just might be some serious consequences. Do the people who unhesitatingly declare themselves atheists not give even a passing thought to the "what if" question? Like what if there *is* a god and she/he/it is mightily offended? Would that be a one-way ticket to a fiery eternity? That's probably–in my opinion– a longshot. But even if there is only a .000000000000001% chance of me burning in hell, that's enough to give me pause.

At the same time, like I said, this whole *nothing* thing is most definitely intriguing. More than intriguing, though. When I consider the idea, I can feel the grip in my solar plexus loosen. My body is talking to me and that's gotta mean something.

For now, this is all on the back burner at a low simmer. Of course, it's probably too late to dive in to any religion with the commitment it would take to have the tenets really take root. And how important is it really to grapple with precisely how to identify myself? "Hi, I'm Liz and I'm an agnostic," or "Hi, I'm Liz and I'm an atheist." Really, is it so important that I figure out which badge to slap on my lapel?

Pascal aside, does it matter?

26

I, IT SEEMS, AM A HUNGRY GHOST

The Buddha teaches us that attachment is the root cause of suffering. So many ways, so many things that we/I can grasp on to, sometimes in the most white-knuckle way. People, ideas, things, experiences. All are capable of an almost magnetic pull. *Dukkha*, that's the Sanskrit word for the main kind of suffering in our lives, suffering that comes from our tendency to grasp and hold on with all our might. We suffer because everything must eventually change and die so all our attempts to cling to them are ultimately futile. As Jack Kornfield said, "Everything that has a beginning has an ending. Make you peace with that and all will be well."

Oh, Jack. Are you saying it's really that easy for you?

Okay, so what must I learn about grasping and attachment? It only took a minute into my research that I came across the idea of *Pretas* or Hungry Ghosts. This is a pretty disturbing concept, guys, mostly because I feel so *seen*, and not in a good way. Hungry Ghosts are beings tormented by desires that can never be sated. In illustrations they have tiny mouths and throats and the swollen bellies of the starving, suggesting that they can never consume enough to ease the suffering of their hungers. Ugh. As if I didn't need more incentive to tackle this attachment to life thing, that visual should be plenty motivating.

If I continue down the Buddhist stream of thought, the only way out is to achieve *Nirvana,* and I don't know about you, but to me that sounds like a steep–no wait–an impossible hill to climb. You want to ease your suffering? Let go of attachment? Reach Nirvana? Okay, then you must:

ACKNOWLEDGE THE FOUR NOBLE TRUTHS

1. the truth of suffering
2. the truth of the cause of suffering
3. the truth of the end of suffering, and
4. the truth of the path that leads to suffering

EXTINGUISH PASSION: completely eliminate desires, cravings and attachments and blow out the fires of passion, greed and hatred

RENOUNCE DESIRE: i.e. stop doing what you want to do just because you desire it

FOLLOW THE NOBLE EIGHTFOLD PATH

1. right view
2. right intention
3. right speech
4. right action

5. right livelihood
6. right effort
7. right mindfulness, and
8. right concentration.

CULTIVATE MORALITY, MEDITATION, AND WISDOM: no explanation needed

APPROACH THE WORLD WITH COMPASSION, PATIENCE, AND JOY: but wait, isn't joy a passion or am I missing something?

CONTEMPLATE THE UNIVERSE THROUGH MEDITATION: okay, I guess I can do that

I leave it to you to explore this path if you so choose. Me? I absolutely, 100%, not a shred of a doubt, know that in a zillion years I could never attain Nirvana if all of that is what's required. And I know myself well enough to understand that a more, shall we say, unconventional—maybe even irreverent—plan of attack is best suited to me.

I don't need the Buddha to convince me that we all need to confront the challenge of letting go. So, so, so many ways. There is not a client I have worked with where this challenge does not raise its not-so-pretty head. The need to let go? Ubiquitous, most definitely. Lifelong? Yes, ma'am. When I talk to clients about letting go, we often identify these challenges:

Emotional discomfort

- Letting go can bring up painful emotions that people may try to avoid, like grief, guilt, or disappointment.

Fear of the unknown

- Releasing something familiar, even if it's not serving you, can create anxiety about what lies ahead.

Identity tied to the past

- Sometimes, people feel like a part of their identity is intertwined with the thing they need to let go of.

Resistance to change

- Humans naturally tend to prefer stability and the familiar so can resist letting go of something even when it is no longer beneficial.

Need for closure

- Sometimes, letting go requires finding a sense of closure in a situation, which can be difficult if there are unresolved issues.

My current tactic is to assume that whatever efforts I make at letting go in whatever areas of my life, will/should ultimately help in the letting go, final frontier-wise.

Here is my status report as of this writing:

Appearance: I'd say I'm about 75% of the way on the rocky road of letting go of my looks. What's left in that 25% is stuff like:

- coloring my gray roots
- putting turquoise highlights in my hair
- getting another tattoo
- passing on dessert
- wearing clothes that verge on being too young
- believing Jane Seymour who is only a few years younger than I when she promises that if I buy the cream she's hawking on TV that it will erase the crepe-y skin on my arms which makes me think of my mother (and not in a good way) any time I look and which has eliminated sleeveless garments from my wardrobe forever
- And finally this: a couple of years ago I went to see an aesthetician for a consultation. I've never been tempted by Botox. Yeah, there are lines but I've never aspired to a face that looks like a marble table top. Even the admittedly deep lines on the sides of my nose...nasolabial as they say in the trade. They don't bother me... much. But Lordy, those melomental folds, also and horrifyingly known as marionette lines (picture Howdy Doody) Those!!!! They seemed to *not* be there one day and then boom! They are all I can see. Those fuckers bother(ed) the shit out of me. So the aesthetician tells me what she can do to take care of those lines and

I can barely stay in the chair while she explains the process. She'd numb me, use a needle to create an entry point and then insert a cannula which is a thin tube that would carry the filler. Are you kidding me, woman? But, she told me the results should last for over a year so okay, fine, let's do it, but please stop talking about it. It was not fun, I can tell you, but I was thrilled with the results. Those lines nearly vanished. A frickin' miracle. The money and pain and gross-out factor totally worth it. But not so fast. After only a day or so, I felt lumps around the area and, to cut to the chase, I apparently had an allergic reaction so had to go back and repeat the nasty process so I could get the filler dissolved. Oh hi, marionette lines. You're back.

Romance: I'm about 99.9% all the way down the road of letting go of romance. You guys should understand how deeply weird it is to have come to this unrecognizable place in my life. A deeply foreign land. Starting at about 13 years old when my best friend Donna and I would decide who would be our boyfriend and then inform the lucky guys, since then until my last husband's death in 1999, the amount of time without a guy, well, too short to even mention. I had always been a boy-crazy chick. So yes, I've had more than my fair share of romance in my life. And along with that more than ample share of romance, I have also had more than my fair share of heartbreak. Yes, I have suffered and recovered and suffered and recovered and etc. and so forth. Yes, I know, the heart is a resilient organ. I am just not sure if at this late date there is any pliancy left in that dusty, desiccated body part of mine. And another thing: it helps that, given my age and the fact that after my bout with breast cancer I had a five-year course of estrogen blockers, well, if there was a single droplet of that particular hormone left in my body, those drugs found it and obliterated it. Libido? What libido.

Control: I'm about 50, maybe 60% along the way of letting go of control. I'm working on it.
Good God, I am doing my best. I could get all professional psychologist here and talk about how a need for control is related to insecure attachments in childhood but really, so what? True or not, and for whatever the etiology, this issue of control has dogged me for as long as I've been an introspective human. The most significant way this shows up in my life is in the neurotic belief that every problem in the lives of those I love is mine to solve, mine to fix. Dear kids and grandchild of mine: this comes as no surprise to you, I am dead certain. While it is so true that the impulse lives on, the actions are dwindling. I may feel the muscle memory of jumping in, but at least half the time I can give myself a good talking to and resist the urge. Write the email but delete it before sending. Silently count to five before opening my mouth. Think twice before I forward that article. The beat goes on but I am so much more aware of this affliction and I am grateful for the gentle (usually) ally that sits on my shoulder, ready to get my attention as I am poised to exert control where I ought not. Working on it. Working on it. Working on it.

My Life on Planet Earth: I am trying my very best. Maybe 30% along the way. My experience with psychedelics moved me down the path; my exploration of panpsychism, that too; confronting what now seems like a rather bizarre imagining of what the after-death experience might look like: floating around in solitary, infinite blackness; glimmers of possibility that there might be something more; my talks with hospice workers; reading reports of near-death experiences; and the sense that there is more to this than simply (!) fear for me, something else at work. I surprise myself as I write this but even the word "fear" seems somehow degraded. Some of the punch drained away. All of this—the whole exploration—has, yes, resulted in some not-so-insignificant progress as I chip away at this Gibraltar-sized boulder. More distance to travel, I know. Ask me again tomorrow.

Postscript: In my family we have a year-end tradition. We each write a note to ourselves, seal it, address it, and stamp it so it can be mailed to us at the end of the following year. Mine says the same thing every year: *Let go!*

27

FAMOUS, ALBEIT OSTENSIBLE, LAST WORDS

"I do not want this soup."
—Philip Roth's mother

"At 50, everyone has the face he deserves."
—George Orwell

"I'm looking for loopholes."
—W.C. Fields

"I am tired of ruling over slaves."
—-Frederick the Great

"This wallpaper is dreadful, one of us will have to go."
—-Oscar Wilde

"Plaudite, amici, comedia finita est. (applaud my friends, the comedy is over)"
—-Ludwig van Beethoven

"I want to go when I want. It is tasteless to prolong life artificially. I have done my share; it is time to go. I will do it elegantly."
—-Albert Einstein

"Hold the cross high so I may see it through the flames!"
—-Joan of Arc

"All my possessions for a moment of time."
—Queen Elizabeth 1

"You will not find me alive at sunrise."
—Nostradamus

"Take away those pillows. I shall need them no more."
—Lewis Carroll

"I hope the exit is joyful and hope never to return"
—Frida Kahlo

"Goodnight my darlings, I'll see you tomorrow"
—Noel Coward

"Leave the shower curtain on the inside of the tub."
—Conrad Hilton

"Everything is an illusion."
—-Mata Hari

"If a bullet should enter my brain, let that bullet destroy every closet door."
—-Harvey Milk

"It's very beautiful out there."
   —-Thomas Edison

"I am not the least afraid to die."
   —-Charles Darwin

"I want nothing but death."
   —-Jane Austen

"A certain butterfly is already on the wing."
   —-Vladimir Nabokov

"I knew it! I knew it! Born in a hotel room and, goddamn it, dying in a hotel room."
   —-Eugene O'Neill

"God bless Captain Vere."
   —-Herman Melville

"It's better to burn out than to fade away."
   —-Kurt Cobain

"Mozart!"
   —-Gustav Mahler

"I'm losing."
   —-Frank Sinatra

"A party! Let's have a party."
   —-Margaret Sanger

"I don't want the doctor's death. I want to have my own freedom."
   —-Rainer Maria Rilke

"Pardonnez-moi, monsieur."
—Marie Antoinette
(after stepping on her executioner's foot)

"God damn the whole friggin' world and everyone in it but you, Carlotta."
—W.C. Fields

"This is no way to live!"
—Groucho Marx

"Good dog."
—Vladimir Ilych Lenin

"I'm bored with it all."
—Sir Winston Churchill

"Mama—Mama—Mama."
—Truman Capote

"Oh wow. Oh wow. Oh wow."
—Steve Jobs

"I'm going to the bathroom to read."
—Elvis Presley

"The taste of death is upon my lips. I feel something that is not of this earth."
—Wolfgang Amadeus Mozart

"Turn up the lights, I don't want to go home in the dark."
—O. Henry

"It is well, I die hard, but I am not afraid to go."
—George Washington

"I just wish I had time for one more bowl of chili."
—Kit Carson

"Lord help my poor soul."
—Edgar Allan Poe

"That was the best ice-cream soda I ever tasted."
—Lou Costello

"This is the last of earth, I am content."
—John Quincy Adams

"I have offended God and mankind because my work didn't reach the quality it should have."
—Leonardo da Vinci

"I've never felt better."
—Douglas Fairbanks, Sr.

"Is it the Fourth?"
—Thomas Jefferson

"Get my swan costume ready."
—Anna Pavlova

"I'd hate to die twice. It's so boring."
—Richard Feynman

"Go on, get out—last words are for fools who haven't said enough."
—Karl Marx,

"The earth is suffocating . . . Swear to make them cut me open, so that I won't be buried alive."
—-Frederic Chopin

"That was a great game of golf, fellers."
—-Bing Crosby

"Don't worry chief, it will be alright."
—-Rudolph Valentino

"Damn it...Don't you dare ask God to help me"
—-Joan Crawford

"Codeine . . . bourbon."
—-Tallulah Bankhead

"I see black light."
—-Victor Hugo

"Does nobody understand?"
—-James Joyce

"How were the receipts today at Madison Square Garden?"
—-P. T. Barnum

"God bless... God damn."
—-James Thurber

"Nothing matters. Nothing matters."
—-Louis B. Mayer

"All is lost. Monks, monks, monks"
—-Henry VIII

"The sadness will last forever."
   —-Vincent Van Gogh

"I'll finally get to see Marilyn."
   —Joe DiMaggio

"See you later, I feel like I'm in good hands."
   —-Jim Henson

"Ow, fuck!"
   —-Roald Dahl

"Thank you."
   —Freddie Mercury

"Help."
   —-Richard Nixon

"Kiss my ass."
   —John Wayne Gacy

"Oh, come on."
   —Kingsley Amis

"Toodle-oo!"
   —Allen Ginsberg

Love one another."
   —George Harrison

"Am I a sheep?"
   —Fred Rogers

"I should have been a concert pianist."
—Edward Teller

"It's time."
—Johnny Cash

"Remember to look up at the stars and not down at your feet."
—Stephen Hawking

"I don't want to die."
—Amy Winehouse

"Capitalism... Downfall."
—Christopher Hitchens

"I'm OK."
—Hugh Hefner

"I'm bored."
—James Baldwin

"Where is my clock?"
—Salvador Dalí

"Utter Nonsense"
—Eleanor Roosevelt

"Every damn fool thing you do in this life you pay for."
—Edith Piaf

"Don't let it end like this. Tell them I said something."
—Pancho Villa

"Back in no time."
—William S. Burroughs

"So here it is at last. The distinguished thing."
—Henry James

"Adieu, mes amis. Je vais à la gloire"
—Isadora Duncan

28

NOTHING NEW UNDER THE SUN

There is this thing I've been thinking about... this reality, or maybe it's an assumption. Maybe it's rational or maybe it's not—I just don't know. What I do know, and what is inescapably true, is that I'm rounding the bend to my ninth decade. If you met me, you might agree that I am young for my age (humble brag), but come on, I could look and act like a zygote, but how many more excursions around that orb do I realistically have? So, this is the belief... or maybe assumption... or maybe intuition that lives in me: nothing new will happen in my life. There will be no surprises. No big ones, at least. Nothing will happen that will knock me back on my heels in a kind of I-sure-didn't-see-that-coming way.

Over the course of my life, I can count—let's see, six? Eight? Whatever the number, there definitely have been some significant examples of careening turns my life has taken. I'm talking here about things that I never could have envisioned. Some good, some amazing, some total shit. All unanticipated.

For example: that time when I was a young mother

living in a place I did not, not, NOT love, and I enrolled in a continuing education course because I was bored, had no goals, no passions, not a moment's thought as to what in the friggin' world I might want to do. It turned out that the woman teaching the class was so lovely, so charismatic, that I ended up asking her about her education and, on what felt like a whim, decided on the spot that, okay, I'll do that too, I'll get that same degree—which, seemingly and miraculously, led to the best possible career for me.

Never could have predicted that.

Or: I'm going merrily along my way, living my quotidian life, when I meet this guy and—flash forward, not even that long, just a matter of mere months—and I'm living in a place so new and different to me that I may as well have needed the *Deluxe Duolingo—American languages version*—to prepare myself for life in this new place.

Yeesh, did not see that coming!

And then the time a routine, annual medical test was followed by a call at 8:30 on a Thursday night from a doctor delivering the bad news, which was an outcome I had naively never anticipated because it was breast cancer—and my sister, who is six years younger, had suffered her own bout several years before, so, in my deluded logic, I assumed I had escaped the danger age.

That particular curveball was not in my plan.

So yes, some of these unpredictable turns have been fabulous, others terrifying and horrible. But bad or good, they have, in fact, been activating. Nothing like a new love affair to stimulate your system (pun intended). That's obvious. But a cancer diagnosis, too—that'll jolt you out of bed and percuss your body. Horrible or wonderful, all of these big, major changes in my life involved energy.

I certainly do not want another cancer diagnosis. And I also do not want another love affair. But when I contend with the belief/assumption/reality that I will not have another *man-I-sure-didn't-see-that-coming!* experience, I get this kind of dulled feeling. Like the rest of my time on earth will be flat and with very little range—just limping along, biding time.

Strange as it sounds—even to me who lived it—a cancer diagnosis comes with a kind of vitality (an ironic word choice, I admit). Moments are heightened, feelings are more acute. Time is measured in minutes. The now is more now than ever. And a new romance? That's when all our cells are firing. Talk about energizing!

On the other hand, when I examine the belief that there are no more significant surprises for me, I get this sense of my remaining time as monotonous and rutted. Flat and lifeless. I don't know about you, but what those two words conjure for me—flat and lifeless—is an ICU unit and the flat-line sound of a monitor registering a heart that has stopped beating.

What an unanticipated awareness this is for me! When I imagine the remainder of my time on earth moving along in a flat and lifeless way—and this is very strange to say—I feel just a teensy bit more ready to call it quits.

HELLO DARKNESS, MY NEW FRIEND

Hollywood portrayals of therapy sessions are often replete with these big Eureka moments—the slap-your-forehead A-HA experiences. To me, this is not only a misrepresentation of the process but a disservice to people who might be considering therapy. And it's also not great for folks who turn to their therapist and demand, "Hey, where's my eye-popping insight?"

I'll tell you where: in that haystack, right near the needle.

Yes, these moments of epiphany happen, but they are rare and not the real progress in therapy, which is—for the most part—effortful, boringly repetitious, and hard-won. Chip, chip, chip.

In my own life on the other side of the couch, I can count two or three dramatic experiences like that in my history as a client—insights that felt so monumental, so enlightening, that they nearly knocked the bejesus out of me. And besides the revelation of it all, I remember being shook up in a "why-the-hell-didn't-I-realize-that?" way. These were insights that went from being completely out of my awareness to blindingly obvious in the space of a moment, and I was definitely tempted to berate myself for being so myopic.

Switching back to my office chair, I can say that it's not uncommon for a client to feel embarrassed when they come to experience something as completely obvious that, just a second ago, was out of their awareness. I get it. It's humbling, for sure. Humbling, but hopefully not humiliating. Of course, these words have the same Latin root: *humilis*, meaning "of the earth." Similarities, for sure, but the emotional tone is so very disparate. I don't know about you, but I can feel the difference in my body—feeling humiliated versus having humility. The times I've felt humiliated, I wanted to cover my face and shrink myself out of sight. It's a terrible feeling. Humility, on the other hand—while also not a barrel of laughs—is about our flawed, shared humanity—not only flawed but unfinished. There will always be things we have to learn about ourselves, and if our response to some new insight is to berate ourselves, well, that is simply a denial of our imperfect humanity.

After all, we only know what we know when we know it. We are not frozen in amber. Of course I have things to learn about myself. I always will. What kind of hubris—and ultimate humiliation—is it to believe that I have reached a point where I know all there is to know about myself? Cuz, come on, there is no finish line where I get to spike the ball and do the victory dance.

These experiences of humility are the price of admission for those of us committed to a life of introspection.

And then there is the concept of readiness. We are ready when we are ready, and it is usually after an accretion of experiences and insights and, frankly, getting tossed about by life. You just can't push the river. Think of filling a glass with water, one drip at a time. That last drip—the one that spills over the edge—only does so on top of all the drips that have come before it. That's how I think of readiness.

And now this moment. After all these months of working on this project—all the drip, drip, drip...

Eureka!

When I started this deep dive, it was my intention to find a way—as skeptical as I was that it might be remotely possible—to ease my fears about my mortality. These two words seemed inextricably bound: death + fear. How could I—how could anyone—separate one from the other?

So dive in I did, looking under every rock. I let myself swim in it all, often feeling all my pulse points pound. That's fear, right?

When I first meet with a client, I ask what brings them in, what it is they want to work on. I listen intently, make notes, and of course I honor their stated intention. That said, I never assume that what they name as their objective is the full story. What I've learned over these many years is that, as earnest as their stated goals might be, almost always, there are deeper needs and motivations. I never think of this as a client avoiding or obfuscating—okay, maybe there is some of that at work. After all, it isn't easy to open up to a complete stranger about your deepest fears and concerns. Respect. It takes time for a therapeutic alliance to form and for a client to know they can trust me.

Even so, I think there is often something less than conscious going on. I've had so many experiences over my life—personally and professionally—that lead me to believe in the wisdom of our unconscious selves. Your conscious mind and stated intention may be wanting help figuring out if you should stay married, while your unconscious mind is motivated to heal the deeper, older wounds of not being parented in the way you should have been, resulting in a core fear of being unlovable. That's one example. Almost always, it takes time and the strengthening of a therapeutic alliance for profound feelings and fears like these to even reach a client's consciousness. So often this is the work of meaningful therapy—getting to the root of it all. A more elegant approach, rather than slapping on a Band-Aid.

All of this is to say that this project has been like a developing therapeutic alliance between me and myself. The safer I felt with myself, the deeper I went, and the more clarity I found. Please believe, I am not here to say that I am now—POOF—fear-free. Not at this moment, at least. If I imagine myself *in extremis*, with no quality of life, maybe full of pain—well, that's another story. I can easily believe there would be no room for fear in that scenario.

So yes, I still carry fear. After all, is there a bigger unknown?

And another thing about fear: I've never been a particularly brave person when it comes to my physical self. I don't love roller coasters; I'm too afraid of the ocean to scuba dive; and I would never, ever, no matter how much you paid me, bungee jump. But take emotional risks? You bet your boots! I'm a gold medal winner on that front, for better and, yessum, for worse. I realize this makes no logical sense—in fact, sounds pretty wacky—but I have filed death under the physical category of endeavor: my just-a-second-ago alive body disappearing into the blackest and most infinite void. The ultimate bungee jump.

There are two different things that have happened, though. First of all, looking at death from every angle has had a dulling effect—and I mean dulling in a good way. It's like exposure therapy. If you're not familiar with this therapeutic method, it's a cognitive-behavioral approach where one is gradually exposed to feared situations and sensations in order to reduce anxiety. The way this approach works—theoretically, at least—is to first establish a safe environment, and then gradually expose the client to fearful stimuli which will, after time and hopefully, challenge their dysfunctional beliefs, after which, ideally, they will learn to tolerate their fear. Chip, chip, chip. Drip, drip, drip. Not that this was my intention going in but, huh, I was actually subjecting myself to exposure therapy.

While at the start of this project I may have deliberately used the word "terror" to describe my feelings toward my mortality, now I feel almost embarrassed to cop to that. Nope, I am not terrified. Maybe you feel that the journey from terror to apprehension is insignificant. Not I. For me, this trip has been around the world and back, two or three times.

So, that was the first—the first and most definitely epic—result of this exploration. But here's the other thing. Maybe you notice this in yourself, that some feelings are easier to access than others. Some people have no trouble feeling and expressing the "harder" emotions, like anger or disdain, but softer feelings like empathy and sadness may be much more of a challenge. We all have feelings we are "better" at. For me, there's not a value judgment in that. Sad but true, our growing-up experiences tend to prune our emotional responses. Certain emotional muscles are strengthened over time and experience, and some are not. As we grow, there will be areas of strength and places in us that are less well-developed. Learn, we must.

Which brings me to this other unexpected outcome. The amount of time I spent looking at this topic from every angle, the more I grappled, the exposure therapy—all of this must have created more of a sense of safety and trust, that same way a client might feel less and less guarded with a trusted therapist. It's about my relationship with myself, really, and how, to my surprise, I let my guard down enough to see what lay beneath the fear. It's a strange inversion of the wolf-in-sheep's-clothing thing, where the sheep is—weird, I know—my fear.

Please believe, I understand how debilitating fear and anxiety can be. And this is not to rank order feelings in merit or quality. But this is *my* Eureka. For good or for bad and for whatever reason, fear is a more practiced emotional response for me. The groove is pretty deep. Fear has tended to be my go-to emotion in stressful situations. This is territory I can navigate blind. Just watch me get to the worst possible outcome in a heartbeat. I take the gold every time. And here I am, after the dulling/exposure effect of working on this project, along with ever-deepening trust in myself, meeting that dang wolf.

Hidden under a defense as near-impervious as plate armor:

- SADNESS
- MELANCHOLY

- SORROW

I have some glimmering insight into my personal challenge of letting this family of feelings take center stage. I understand how my unconscious has been at work. Thanks for that, old friend. I understand why that was helpful at the time. But whatever the antecedents, the truth remains. Fear has been easier for me. Tears, not so much. Even after my beloved husband died—of course I was sad; of course I cried for hours at a time. AND, I remember this panicked, fearful voice in my head saying, "What am I going to do? What am I going to do?"

Sorrow is a soul-deep pain that I have kept as far out of reach as possible. If you take sadness to the farthest end, that's where you'll find sorrow. It's no wonder I'd want to avoid going there—to avoid and then moor myself to fear instead, rather than deeply grapple with the yawning sadness that will be with me at the end.

My beloved grandson is 17 at this writing. It is such a profound ache I feel when I let myself really know—truly let it sink in—that I will not be here to see what kind of full-grown man he becomes. Doubtful I will live long enough to see what kind of family he forms. And if he has children, who will they be? In all likelihood, I will never know. And I will not be here to help him. And how will my own children's journeys unfold? I doubt that their later lives will look like they do now, and my heart breaks because I will not be there to witness and to share. Even the hard times, I'll miss those too. I will not be here to help and comfort them in their later lives when/if they struggle. And I won't be here as they gather with extended family for holidays, which I so dearly hope they do. All the Thanksgivings, the family birthdays, the game nights. Even my dog—what if I die before him, leaving him confused and feeling abandoned?

But here I am, in a place that is more true, at least for me. And truer = more honest = braver = better. I do believe that Shakespeare was right: "Give sorrow words; the grief that does not speak whispers the o'erfraught heart and bids it break."

Is this the most obvious thing to the rest of you, that it's about what we will miss when we're gone? And, if so, I wish you'd have told me so I could have released at least some of my fear sooner.

But here I am with this new awareness taking root, and what a strange thing—being grateful to have arrived here.

Hello darkness, my new friend.

30

RELATIONSHIP STATUS

Querida Santa Muerta:
I want you to know that I am re-evaluating our relationship. It's not that I'm breaking up with you–even if I could, which, of course, I can't. Duh! I accept that we are bound together, or maybe it's more accurate to say that I am in *process*; I am working on it. I am accept*ing* that we are inextricably tied together.

I am not on some quixotic endeavor here. Stupid I am not. Naive, nope. Not even deluded. I know there is no *me* without *you*.

But. My feelings toward you have changed.

Let me try and explain.

Maybe you'll be flattered to know about all the research I did about you. Consider yourself seen. There were some mighty dark alleys I went down and in my travels, I encountered some pretty scary shit and there was definitely icky stuff too. To be fair, though, you should know that I did find a modicum of comfort as well. Maybe more than a modicum, actually. Let me give myself the credit I deserve. It's in my body, the change I can feel. How I am not so likely to automatically feel my body go into fight or flight when I speak your name. That's a change, I hope you can agree.

Here's what I know: I am grateful for this deep dive exploration. Yes, as I said, some of what I've read and learned has been scary. Some has been icky. I may have just as many questions as I had before. Even so, I am grateful. At this late stage in life I may have much more white matter in this brain of mine but still I am committed to prying open the places in my mind that have been shut tight. Every step deeper into this exploration has released my hold on certainty, tiny bit by tiny bit; has decreased my fear, nano-bit by nano-bit. And you know how it is, when you're making tiny steps toward a goal, how it's sometimes hard to recognize your progress? This is me, reminding myself. Giving myself credit. Reinforcing my efforts.

Baby steps, y'all. Baby steps.

Things that have shifted and given me some comfort:

- If I am in hospice care, I may just be more ready to let go than I can imagine from this relatively healthy vantage point. And I do believe that whatever hospice workers tend to my care–if I am lucky enough to have hospice workers tend to my care–they will be gentle-voiced and kind and committed to shepherding me on my way.
- When I think about annihilation and oblivion–the concepts that have created the most fear in me–I now remind myself that there is a difference between *something* and *nothing*; that the picture I've held–as bizarre and outlandish as it sounds when I actually cop to it–is me floating around in the blackest of blackness for eternity. And that picture is a picture of

something. On the other hand, when I think of what it/I was before I was born, what I imagine is *nothing*. And *nothing* just might be nothing to be afraid of.
- I'm about 90% convinced of the ubiquity of consciousness. And I believe in physics: according to the law of the conservation of mass, matter cannot be destroyed, it can only change form. I can't get anywhere close to believing that any "Liz-ness" will remain when I'm gone but just try and permanently get rid of this bag of bones and organs and tissue. Go ahead and try to defy the laws of physics!
- Terror has given way to fear which has given way to something deeper, more true. How profoundly sad I will be that I will not be here to see how things unfold for my beloved family. Fear, I want to run from. Sorrow, that I can live (HA!) with. Not because it's easier, because NO! But because it is more unambiguously true.

So where does this leave us, you and me? For starters, I don't like having enemies. And actual enemies? Not sure I've had any. Yes, to be sure, I've had friendships that have gone sideways and don't get me started on husbands. But in this long life of mine, I have been deeply unsettled when a relationship has even approximated the enemy status. It was like an invisible weight that I dragged around until the relationship shifted to something more benign...former friends, maybe. Someone I wouldn't need to cross the street to avoid.

You, though—before this whole exploration I have considered you my mortal enemy. HA! *Mortal enemy*! How on the nose!

So, *Muerta* AKA *mort* AKA *shi* AKA *morte* AKA *tod* AKA *dood* AKA *al-moat* AKA 死 AKA *smert* AKA Θάνατος AKA *mawt*:

Where does this leave us? My erstwhile bête noire. Today, maybe not my enemy but to call you a friend? What's true is that I no longer feel the need to cross the street when I see you coming. But friends? How I'd ever travel that far is inconceivable to me. Truth is, there is not enough life left for me to move far enough on the path of enlightenment to call you my friend. For sure you are a constant companion. Yes, you will be with me for the distance. Yes, we are in it for the long haul, bound together. You, I am forced to admit, have accompanied me on this journey from near-terror to near-acceptance. But my friend? Nope. I'm thinking the best I can do is to consider you my friendly rival. Yes, that, I do believe, I can do.

With respect,
Liz

AFTERWORD

There used to be 27 letters in the English alphabet. In the 18th and early 19th century, this was the alphabet:

A B C D E F G H I J K L M N O P Q R S T U V W X Y Z
   and the symbol, &

Originally, before *ampersand* was a word, this was read as "...X Y Z "*and, per se, 'and'*"
   Which is a rather complicated way of saying that the symbol & means *and* (Over time *and, per se, and* was re-bracketed to become the word *ampersand*.)
   I'm not sure I've ever been quite as aware of the power of that one simple word.
   What a difference when you end an alphabet or a sentence or a thought or a life with and...

What a difference when you end an alphabet or
a sentence or
a thought or
a life with
and...

DEATH BE NOT PROUD

Death, be not proud, though some have called thee
Mighty and dreadful, for thou art not so;
For those whom thou think'st thou dost overthrow
Die not, poor Death, nor yet canst thou kill me.
From rest and sleep, which but thy pictures be,
Much pleasure; then from thee much more must flow,
And soonest our best men with thee do go,
Rest of their bones, and soul's delivery.
Thou art slave to fate, chance, kings, and desperate men,
And dost with poison, war, and sickness dwell,
And poppy or charms can make us sleep as well
And better than thy stroke; why swell'st thou then?
One short sleep past, we wake eternally
And death shall be no more; Death, thou shalt die.

—John Donne

Liz Scott, Ph.D.

Liz is a psychologist in private practice. Her memoir, *This Never Happened*, came out in 2019 followed by *Love Life: Confessions of a Psychologist* in 2024. Originally from New York, she lives and works in Portland, Oregon

Acknowledgments

Enormous gratitude to Kurt and *Pierian Springs Press* for believing in this pretty weird project.

And to Shavaun Scott, my publishing housemate, endless thanks for your advocacy and support.

Gigi Little, what can I say? You are always the most generous of resources.

Doug Chase, deepest thanks for your patience with all my questions.

Thanks to Rene Denfeld, Courtenay Hameister, Jennifer Pastiloff, Michelle Wildgen, Shoshanna Ungerleider, Suzy Vitello, Anne Gudger, E.B. Bartels, Laura Stanfill and Shavaun Scott for your willingness to read and blurb. Believe me, I understand the bigness of the ask.

Bottom of my heart gratitude to the *Dangerous Writers* for supporting the baby writer in me and to my beloved *Henry Writers* for years of encouragement and help beyond measure.

To Kathleen Lane: prayer hands and a zillion hearts for our years of friendship and the many bushels of bananas.

For Tom Spanbauer, wherever you are: without you, none of this.

Mac and Billy: In an ideal world you would understand what you bring to my life.

Ashley, Erica and Milo: loving you is my meaning.

www.ingramcontent.com/pod-product-compliance
Lightning Source LLC
LaVergne TN
LVHW090041080526
838202LV00046B/3909